Mastering Organizational Knowledge Flow

WILEY & SAS BUSINESS SERIES

The Wiley & SAS Business Series presents books that help senior-level managers with their critical management decisions.

Titles in the Wiley and SAS Business Series include:

Business Intelligence Competency Centers: A Team Approach to Maximizing Competitive Advantage by Gloria J. Miller, Dagmar Brautigam, and Stefanie Gerlach

Business Intelligence Success Factors: Tools for Aligning Your Business in the Global Economy by Olivia Parr Rud

Case Studies in Performance Management: A Guide from the Experts by Tony C. Adkins

CIO Best Practices: Enabling Strategic Value with Information Technology by Joe Stenzel

Credit Risk Assessment: The New Lending System for Borrowers, Lenders, and Investors by Clark Abrahams and Mingyuan Zhang

Credit Risk Scorecards: Developing and Implementing Intelligent Credit Scoring by Naeem Siddiqi

Customer Data Integration: Reaching a Single Version of the Truth by Jill Dyché and Evan Levy

Demand-Driven Forecasting: A Structured Approach to Forecasting by Charles Chase

Enterprise Risk Management: A Methodology for Achieving Strategic Objectives by Gregory Monahan

Fair Lending Compliance: Intelligence and Implications for Credit Risk Management by Clark R. Abrahams and Mingyuan Zhang

Information Revolution: Using the Information Evolution Model to Grow Your Business by Jim Davis, Gloria J. Miller, and Allan Russell

Marketing Automation: Practical Steps to More Effective Direct Marketing by Jeff LeSueur

Performance Management: Finding the Missing Pieces (to Close the Intelligence Gap) by Gary Cokins

Performance Management: Integrating Strategy Execution, Methodologies, Risk, and Analytics by Gary Cokins

The Data Asset: How Smart Companies Govern Their Data for Business Success by Tony Fisher

The New Know: Innovation Powered by Analytics by Thornton May

Visual Six Sigma: Making Data Analysis Lean by Ian Cox, Marie A. Gaudard, Philip J. Ramsey, Mia L. Stephens, and Leo Wright (Publishing December 2009)

For more information on any of the above titles, please visit **www.wiley.com**.

Mastering Organizational Knowledge Flow

How to Make Knowledge
Sharing Work

Frank Leistner

WILEY

John Wiley & Sons, Inc.

For general information on our other products and services or for technical support, please contact our Customer Care Department within the United States at (800) 762-2974, outside the United States at (317) 572-3993 or fax (317) 572-4002.

Wiley also publishes its books in a variety of electronic formats. Some content that appears in print may not be available in electronic books. For more information about Wiley products, visit our web site at www.wiley.com.

Library of Congress Cataloging-in-Publication Data

Leistner, Frank.
   Mastering organizational knowledge flow : how to make knowledge sharing work / Frank Leistner.
      p. cm.—(Wiley & SAS business series)
   Includes bibliographical references and index.
   ISBN 978-0-470-55990-1 (cloth)
   1. Knowledge management.   I. Title.
   HD30.2.L453 2010
   658.4'038–dc22

                                                                    2009050975

Printed in the United States of America

10 9 8 7 6 5 4 3 2 1

To my father, who taught me by example that optimism should be a guiding principle for anything you do

Contents

Foreword:
The Generations
of Knowledge
Management

Sometime in the early 1990s, the idea caught on in several organizations that it was actually possible to do something about knowledge in their organizations. The "something" that could be done was often hotly debated among the knowledge practitioners, consultants, academics, and internally competing functions. However, a general consensus emerged by the middle of the decade that could be summarized in this way:

- Knowledge in organizations is most likely to be found in existing or emergent documents.
- The key to managing these documents are better systems— either technology systems or cleverer taxonomies.
- Incentives can easily be developed to encourage the production and use of these documents.
- All of these activities can be measured for their effectiveness within the organization and their costs can be justified this way.
- Knowledge was the result of individual action and thinking and the individual is the most efficient unit of analysis for working with knowledge in the firm.
- Knowledge management projects had a very strong technological component.

These general ideas were termed *knowledge management* (KM) by many (including myself, alas), and by 1995 these ideas had taken hold and much effort and expenditures were being burned up in putting them into practice. Ideas have consequences and these surely did as knowledge practitioners, consultants, and technology vendors all jumped on the KM bandwagon to implement these systems.

Unfortunately, the ideas were flawed. They were not so much wrong as misguided in their approach. Since almost all new movements build on the skeletons of earlier movements, KM looked very much like information management, and, not surprisingly, the results produced by these new KM projects were quite similar to earlier KM projects—disappointing the knowledge advocates and especially the users and clients who were expecting great things from the more effective use of knowledge within the organization.

However, rather then admitting defeat and leaving the field, practitioners rethought many of their assumptions and came up, again with the help of consultants and academics, with some new working hypotheses that seemed much closer to the reality of how knowledge actually works in organizations.

Needless to say, this was not the case for all KM projects. Many stuck with the old models and some still do. But it can be fairly said that these retro efforts almost all became absorbed into more traditional information technology projects and lost their focus and user enthusiasm. They are still fading from sight.

What were some of these new assumptions?

- Knowledge can be best understood as a social phenomenon, and efforts to work with it are better structured as some group effort than by individuals.

- Working with knowledge needs some mixture or combination of technology, strategy, human capital, and social capital approaches.

- It is almost impossible to effectively measure knowledge, and it is not worth the effort to do so.

- A holistic approach is therefore called for—difficult as this may be to formulate and implement.

Luckily for practitioners, there are more than a few people who are offering guides on how to go about doing this. This book you are reading represents one of the clearest and most comprehensive attempts at getting one's hands around this most elusive and valuable resource: organizational knowledge.

Frank Leistner is a true hybrid: a practitioner who has read all the important texts and has thought long and hard about how to go about working with knowledge. He has had the good fortune to have worked for an organization that believes both in using knowledge well and in developing new knowledge. Frank has seen his ideas put into action and has had been able to evaluate them in practice. His ideas are holistic, comprehensive, and, most important, grounded in practice.

All readers should be able to make use of these ideas and continue on the journey of making better use of what we know and how we can know new things.

LARRY PRUSAK
Visiting Professor
Copenhagen Business School

Preface

Many organizations still struggle to make best use of the knowledge that exists within them. While individuals might use their knowledge on a daily basis and for their decisions, frequently that knowledge is not shared and leveraged across the organization from one person to another. A common notion of how to make this transfer of knowledge happen is via technical systems. Those systems play a role as an enabler, but they are only one piece of the puzzle to make the flow of knowledge work in an organization. This book looks at the other factors that are involved and specifically focuses on human aspects. What motivates people to share their knowledge, and how can you overcome some of the barriers that are in the way of a good flow of knowledge in your organization? How should you deal with measuring? What are some of the best drivers that you can put in place not only to get a knowledge flow initiative started but to make sure it survives and can provide longer-term value?

When I started my first initiative (named ToolPool) back in 1997, it was purely to solve a very specific business problem: to leverage technical tools, tips, and tricks around a global organization. Over the years, it turned out that lasting success was based on a lot of factors of which the technical infrastructure was actually a smaller piece than anticipated. I was fortunate enough to get management support to pursue a number of approaches that helped drive ToolPool to what it eventually became. I was also fortunate enough to have a great team that understood the key principles and invested their energy and passion into driving it to success.

Over the last decade I have used a number of the lessons learned and applied them to a range of initiatives designed to improve the knowledge flow at my current company. The more I recognized patterns of what worked and what did not and the more I discussed those findings with others interested in making knowledge flow better, the clearer it became that putting the key findings into a book would be a good idea. Whenever I presented the ideas at internal meetings, external conferences, or company keynotes, the feedback was positive and spawned many fruitful discussions.

During the winter holidays leading into 2009 I came to the conclusion that this might be the year to get started. The end result of the effort offers you 10 chapters of experiences, lessons learned, examples, and stories to illustrate the main key success factors.

Chapter 1 sets the stage with clarifying some of the terminology used. It also introduces what I understand as a holistic view of managing the flow of knowledge. At the end of the chapter the main case study used in the book, ToolPool, is introduced.

Chapter 2 discusses a number of elements that are important to see clearly before starting or in the early phase of launching an initiative. What should the support organization look like? What are some of the key questions you need to ask before you start?

Chapter 3 takes a closer look at a number of roles that participants will or should play over the lifetime of an initiative.

Chapter 4 discusses passionate initiative support, culture, and trust and how they influence the success of enhancing the knowledge flow.

Chapter 5 goes deeper into some of the main drivers for success. How can you use marketing not only to get started but to sustain an initiative? What are some of the ways to grow an initiative and keep your participants motivated to contribute to it?

Chapter 6 takes a different angle by looking at barriers that might be hindering the flow of knowledge and giving a range of examples and solutions on how it might be possible to reduce those barriers.

Chapter 7 looks at the role of technology and how too much focus on technology will endanger your initiative. It also introduces new ways to look at technology and its role within the knowledge flow.

Chapter 8 offers some lessons learned around measuring your initiative. How should you measure? What are some of the key indicators you might want to use? It also looks at the limits of measuring and why you should be very careful with using measures as drivers.

Chapter 9 attempts a cautious look into the future. What are some of the platforms that will play a role in how people share their knowledge in the years to come? Based on the role that Web 2.0 technologies and related processes play, some trends are discussed.

Chapter 10 concludes with some final thoughts and a pointer to a place where further discussion might happen.

At the end of the book you will find Appendix A: Key Success Factors. This list collects the main clarifications and specificactions to take into account in order to tackle issues that you encounter within areas like marketing, barriers, measuring, and motivation.

As the areas of knowledge flow management are steadily evolving, the chapters in this book can only cover a subset of all the issues you might encounter on your way to master the knowledge flow in your organization. But most of the principles are general enough to be applied even after technology has evolved and social processes have changed. The key is to keep a holistic view, spend considerable and persistent effort to manage all those aspects that are directly connected to human behavior, and see technology as the enabler but not as the sole solution.

Acknowledgments

The actual writing of the book was only a very small part of developing the ideas behind it. It was a much longer process, and many people have contributed over the years. The first person I want to thank is Gloria Miller, my manager back in 1997, who gave me the freedom to pursue this somewhat unusual project I had in mind. A lot of credit for developing a "knowledge management" mind goes to those leading and participating in the IBM Institute for Knowledge Management. During my participation from 1999 to 2003, I was fortunate to meet David Snowden, Eric Lesser, Mike Fontaine, Rob Cross, Don Cohen, Steven Denning, and many others. Larry Prusak's great story-filled keynotes were highlights during that time, lighting my own passion for the topic. In combination with the numerous discussions I had with those from other organizations (ranging from the U.S. Army to the World Bank), I always returned home filled with the ideas and energy needed to push forward on my own initiatives. If you get started with knowledge management, you can easily feel somewhat isolated. So reaching out to experts outside your own organization is very important.

The next group that gave me that type of inspiration was the Harvard Learning Innovation Laboratory (LILA). Special thanks go to David Perkins and Daniel Wilson, who invited me to LILA and led such an exceptional group of practitioners and researchers. Robin Athey, Brigitte Lippmann, Carlota Vollhardt, Fred Vail, Peter Engström, Nat Welch, and Mike Prevou are only a few of those to whom I am very thankful for ideas and feedback. I also met Etienne Wenger again at LILA after listening to him at what I consider my first *real* knowledge management presentation at a Chicago conference in 1998. It was great to be able to personally discuss it with him at LILA meetings. I want to thank Tom Davenport for inviting me to the Babson Working Knowledge Research Center, where I met a group of people from whom I learned so much. At Babson I was able to reconnect with Larry Prusak and a number of the IKM members; I also met a range of very inspiring knowledge management thinkers, like Book Manville.

In the last few years I connected with knowledge management groups in Germany and Switzerland. Thanks for some great discussions to Gerold Riempp, Stefan Smolnik, and Reimar Palte from the European Business School and to Beat Knechtli, Olivier Zaech, and Pavel Kraus from the Swiss Knowledge Management forum.

A special thanks goes to my team at SAS, who helped me get the main initiatives off the ground and give their input and feedback: Britta Lerch, Ana Lopez-Echevarria, Victoria Vaca, Paul Higgins, Kerstin Lambert, Anja Häse, Nic Handschuh, Stephanie Salomo, Meike Kalkowsky, and Daniel Kummer. My frequent discussions with Louise Smith, our knowledge manager for the Asia-Pacific region, have been invaluable over the years. Curt Yeo in the United States played a similar role for some time. I also want to thank my dear friend Thomas Bock, who not only provided me with a "sales view" but also served as a great devil's advocate at many occasions.

Especially when writing a book as a single author, it is very important to have good reviewers. A big thank-you for great comments goes to Hannu Ritvanen, Rasmus Staerke, David Biesack, Dee Stribling, and others. Thank you to Holger Ideler for offering me a banking perspective on the topic in a number of pizza sessions here in Zürich. As I am not a native English speaker, John Kohl's book *The Global English Style Guide* proved to be very useful.

Thank you to Stacey Hamilton, my editor at SAS, who led me very smoothly through this adventure of writing my first book and provided such a great interface to Wiley, the publisher. Thanks to all those at Wiley who made it happen. I am also grateful to Scott Isaacs for supporting the idea of the book and giving me the opportunity to start the project.

Last but not least, a really big thank-you goes to my family. My wife, Inge, not only allowed me to vanish weekend after weekend and even holiday time behind the Mac but also gave a lot of moral support over all those years. And my college-age daughters, Alexandra and Franziska, did the same via video-calls from a number of places around Europe.

Mastering Organizational Knowledge Flow

CHAPTER 1

The Human Touch

*The mind is not a vessel to be filled but a fire
to be kindled.*

—Plutarch, AD 46–120, Greek essayist

S ydney, Australia: Brian, a young programmer who recently started with the company, opens up the contribution form for ToolPool, a global system for sharing technical knowledge. He enters some text describing a program he recently wrote based on his knowledge of a programming language he had learned at the university. His program extends one of the core company products in a smart and unusual way.

Madrid, Spain: Isabel, an experienced consultant, is working on a project at a Spanish bank, where she faces an interesting requirement. She visits ToolPool and after a quick search finds and downloads Brian's program, as it will help fulfill the requirement quickly and elegantly. After using it, she goes back to ToolPool and rates Brian's entry with five stars and adds a comment about how much it helped her.

Cary, North Carolina, United States: Mary, the development manager for the product that Brian extended, scans the Monday morning e-mail from ToolPool, finds Brian's program, and adds a link to the wiki page used for planning the next release of the product.

These are examples of what has been known as knowledge management. Unfortunately, very often the analysis of this situation would now go on to talk about what ToolPool is, what technology it was built on, how much it cost to implement it, and how many information technology (IT) people are currently needed to run it.

But what is really happening here is not that Brian's knowledge is being managed. If anything is managed in this process, it is the flow of Brian's knowledge to other relevant parts of the organization. And ToolPool is only one way that this could have happened. Equally, it could have been that Isabel met Brian at an international technical workgroup and found out about his program.

This book is not about knowledge management technology. It is about ways to influence organizational knowledge flow. Technology does play a role as an enabler, and I mention aspects of it, but the focus is on the human side of making knowledge sharing work. How can you motivate people to share their knowledge, if at all? How can you ensure they will continue to participate? What type of incentives should you use? What are some of the barriers inhibiting the flow that you will have to overcome? What can you do to retain the knowledge that exists only in the minds of those leaving your organization?

While I include examples and case studies from an IT company, many of the principles equally apply to any type or form of organization, whether a government agency, a hospital, or a loose group of physiotherapists exchanging their knowledge in some organized fashion. So the word *organization* is to be seen as wider than a single legal entity or company.

WHY THIS BOOK?

If you currently search for books on knowledge management (KM),[1] you will find a lot of them out there. Amazon.com returns about 16,000 results when you search for the combined term. These books range from highly academic ones to hands-on manuals. So why would you need another one? Why did I even consider writing one with all that coverage out there?

Over the years, I have had many discussions on the topic of knowledge sharing and how to make it work in an organization.

When I started my first knowledge exchange initiative (ToolPool) back in 1997, it was not specifically labeled knowledge management, but after a couple more years and through my involvement with the IBM Institute for Knowledge Management (IKM), it became clear that what we were doing would fit into one of the definitions of KM.

ToolPool, this first initiative, is used as the main case study in the book. It is still running very strongly with global participation internally to SAS (the business analytics company for which I work). At almost 13 years, it might be one of the longest-running KM initiatives. By definition, ToolPool is about technical knowledge, but the principles that make it work are highly nontechnical, as you will see. The contrast of technical and nontechnical elements makes it quite suitable as an example.

ToolPool is only one out of a whole range of different KM initiatives, but it was the major experimentation playground for many years. It was the one to observe, adapt, and analyze. ToolPool has a clear focus on sharing technical tips, tricks, tools, and program code. That topical focus made it easier to deduce learnings and lessons learned from it than from a big-bang all-encompassing knowledge base. As it turns out, this focus is already one of its key success factors. As discussed in Chapter 2, big-bang approaches will have a harder time surviving.

Learning through experimentation was paired with learning through interaction with those responsible in other organizations for getting knowledge to flow. Many insights of what works and what does not came through interaction with others, such as colleagues or those whom I met at external organizations, such as the IKM, the Harvard Learning Innovations Laboratory, or the Babson Working Knowledge program. Key notes from KM pioneers such as Larry Prusak and Tom Davenport influenced my thinking as much as break, lunch, and dinner conversations during those events or with colleagues at SAS.

Most of the time it was not about getting tips but sharing experiences and the reaction and discussion that followed. In one case, I was not sure whether I should add ratings to contributions and discussed some of my thoughts around it. It would have been almost impossible to really share *everything* I had on my mind about the issue, as it included a considerable amount of context that was tacit and only in my head.

As always with like-minded people, the learning was reciprocal. I shared key information that others would integrate into their context to come to a new level of understanding, and I received feedback that would take my thinking to the next level and help me realize better strategies to approach complex issues. In the case of ratings, I concluded that they would make sense to explore as long as I created the right environment and made them very practical.

I think it is very important to draw the line between knowledge and information. Knowledge is connected to all the prior experiences and exists only in the context of the mind. It cannot be managed. What can be managed are ways to enable the flow of that knowledge to others. What can be passed is information (data in context), not knowledge.

I was inspired to put my ideas on knowledge sharing into a book by those who experienced the passion that I developed for the topic, whenever I got into one of the frequent discussions around it.[2] And some specifically suggested sharing my recent ideas around the flow of knowledge to a wider audience by publishing them.

Adding to my motivation to write this book was the realization that KM as an organizational discipline has been around for almost two decades, is still acknowledged to be a key factor for organizational success in the future, but often just does not work. A pattern seems to be that those driving it are sometimes doing so based on incorrect assumptions.

Reading and scanning books, articles, or just Twitter messages on KM, I also felt a growing frustration that too much of what has been written focuses on technology. Typically authors talk about "KM Systems" as if you could manage knowledge in a system. And if you look closely, authors frequently mix the words *knowledge* and *information* as if they were synonyms. Often it seems that technology is the only part the authors really understand very well. Other topics that are much closer related to humans are largely neglected. While the author might acknowledge that humans play a central role in KM, often the focus remains on technology.

It is a little bit as if you have a hammer in your hand and then suddenly everything looks like a nail to you. But without understanding and acknowledging the basic difference between the concepts of knowledge and information, you are very likely to use a hammer when you need a razor-sharp knife. In the best case, you just do not get the full benefits from your initiative; in the worst case, you are actually wasting huge amounts of money doing so.

So what is different about this book? I am raising the question of why, with so much expertise (and thousands of books) on the topic, there are still many organizations that struggle with KM. Why can they not make it work? Why is KM not embedded into the everyday practice of every organization if it is so strategic? Why does almost everybody that I talk to tell me that their organization is struggling with making use of existing knowledge? Why is it so hard? I am not claiming that at SAS we have solved all these issues, but we are definitely ahead of the game in many respects.

This book provides some answers to those questions. It might not give you solutions to all potential problems, but it will provide some important reasons why KM might have not worked in your organization and help you with some proven ideas that will make success a lot more likely going forward. According to the Economist Intelligence Unit,[3] knowledge management is one of the five key trends that will determine competitiveness in the coming decade. The other four trends are globalization, demographics, atomization, and personalization.

Some of the ideas and lessons presented here might prove priceless, as they will help you avoid some simple traps and focus on elements to improve the organizational knowledge flow that you might not have thought of or tried in the past.

The remainder of this chapter sets the stage by introducing some terms and basic principles to be discussed later in the book.

I do not provide an extensive set of models or research. Enough books out there cover that.[4] The next chapters contain pragmatic tips and tricks extracted from real-life experiences. The information comes from the front, where initiatives really worked and produced extensive value. The stories and examples presented here come from initiatives that survived the critical starting stages and are continuing to prove themselves after more than a decade.

To set a base-level understanding, I start out with a short discussion of the term *knowledge management*. You will notice that the title of the book contains the term *Knowledge Flow* instead of *Knowledge Management*. I strongly believe that one of the main reasons why KM projects fail is somewhat due to the use of the term knowledge management and the misunderstanding it creates in the mind of stakeholders. The approaches that people take are often guided, or should I say misguided, by starting out with the wrong frame of mind.

Who is the intended audience for this book? For one, it is aimed at those who have been challenged to bring a new organizational knowledge management program to success or revive an existing underperforming one. The stakeholders might be from IT, from a human resources function, from a business unit, or in a strategic role already focused on knowledge like a chief knowledge officer. They might be line function or sponsoring stakeholders like a chief information officer or the head of personnel.

Because executive buy-in and leadership is a major success factor in driving organizational knowledge flows, it is also important that chief executive officers (CEOs) have the proper understanding as they get involved with strategies. After all, the CEOs are the ones who put the topic high on the future agendas of their organizations.

Knowledge management in the current understanding is often seen as a very technical, software-oriented area, and some people see it as relevant for high-tech organizations only, exclusively for those knowledge workers who spend most of their time online.

With the wider view I am taking, I claim that managing knowledge flows is something that can be applied and used in almost any type of organization. If you detach yourself from the idea that it is about storing "knowledge" in a database, you will see that it is applicable to you, even if you work in an environment that sees itself as being highly nontechnical. Some principles will even work for a group of physiotherapists sharing their experiences in various ways, such as in workshops, expert circles, and online forums.

TERMINOLOGY AND DEFINITIONS

About 15 years ago, the term *knowledge management* was starting to be used in organizational environments, and although I had been dealing with activities that would fit a number of the many KM definitions, we did not call it that at the very start. The first initiatives around exchange of knowledge at SAS were dubbed "supporting sharing of what people know"; we did not use the term *knowledge management* until about 1998. Out in the industry the term had quickly been adopted by management consultants and certain software organizations. Suddenly a "database" was a "knowledge base," and any product only remotely connected to helping with influencing the flow of knowledge was given that new "cool" label.

But the hype created a number of issues with the term, and in the end the term got "burned" to a certain degree. The problem was that knowledge is a wide concept, so it was easy to drop anything into it. But using a term for something too unspecific has a number of effects—for instance:

- Everybody makes up their own definition of it.
- It ends up encompassing elements that were never meant to be covered.
- It creates a wrong sense of understanding, and people will use unsuitable approaches to solve issues connected with it.

This is precisely what happened with the term *knowledge management*. So let us have a look at the term in more detail.

First, there is a problem with those two words in combination. If you take a puristic view, it describes something impossible. As Larry Prusak and other KM experts have pointed out, knowledge is actually connected to people, it cannot be managed outside of people's heads. It exists only in the context of prior human experience. So correctly spoken, it is not possible to "manage" that knowledge.[5]

Second, knowledge is actually tacit (implicit) by nature. Nonaka and Takeuchi had talked in their SECI model about ways of externalizing knowledge,[6] but still, once it is outside of people's heads, it is mere information, not knowledge anymore. It actually needs another human being to interpret, internalize, connect, and apply it to actually become knowledge again. Along those same lines, it is not possible to "transfer knowledge," at least not in the direct sense of transferring an entity from one person to another. What actually happens is that person A shares some information, which is then used by person B and combined with prior (tacit) knowledge and experiences to *create* new knowledge. The knowledge is never transferred directly, as that would indicate that it is moving unmodified. It will always change, however. The knowledge that person A had while sharing information and experiences might be somewhat similar to what person B re-creates out of that shared information, but it will always be different, because the framework and the context of prior knowledge and experiences will be different. The word *transfer* indicates the movement of an entity, but that is definitely not what is happening.

A third situation where the word *knowledge* is actually out of place is in the connection with systems, or knowledge bases. The use of the word in that context seems to indicate that knowledge can be stored outside of humans, for example, in a computer system.

One could argue the difference is marginal, but in my mind the fact that knowledge is often seen as an entity that is external to human beings is the number-one reason that so-called knowledge management projects have failed. It easily leads to people using the terms *knowledge, information,* and sometimes even *data* as synonyms.

Based on the previous discussions, you can very easily spot articles or books that talk about knowledge management without the proper understanding. I usually stop reading once I find that authors are mixing the terms *information* and *knowledge* as if they were the same thing. For me that is a clear indication that they do not understand what knowledge is. Try it for yourself: The next time a proclaimed KM expert mixes the terms interchangeably in the introduction to an article, a blog entry, or even a book, I advise you to be careful with the rest of it.

Along the same lines, terms like *knowledge management software* or *knowledge management vendor* are somewhat dangerous. Yes, in the holistic process of managing the knowledge flow, certain tools (be it software or other) play an important enabler role, but to say that you can manage knowledge with software would be similar to talking about *motivation software* or a *motivation vendor*.

So what about Business Intelligence and Business Analytics? Since Business Intelligence and Business Analytics are core offerings of SAS, I have looked into that question for quite some time. Personally I do not regard Business Intelligence or Business Analytics as being part of knowledge flow management. I see those at the feeding end of the knowledge flow. They are technologies that are important in today's organizations in the knowledge discovery and knowledge creation phase. They provide the basis for individuals to develop the type of knowledge that is worth flowing through the organization. Technologies that are getting growing attention include data and text mining. Those are not only increasingly important in the knowledge discovery field but are also used for building ontologies and categorizations, which can be helpful for information structuring. These are all important related topics, but for the sake of success on the key of knowledge flow I would not include them into knowledge flow management.

I hope you have followed my line of thinking so far. I acknowledge that there are alternative ways of looking at these issues. Products and solutions being offered by "KM vendors" can provide considerable value. But they are not managing knowledge. They are enablers to the knowledge flow. The information they process, store, and provide can be used to create new knowledge. Information stored in systems and repositories can be seen as representing "pointers to the one who knows." If those using them do understand it in that way, they will be much more likely to actually go beyond the system and see the value of the knowledge that is behind that information, connected to the human who contributed the "pointer."

Many people do not get the subtle difference and immediately jump to the conclusion that you can manage the actual knowledge in those systems. As a result, the selected approaches to drive the initiatives around them (if there is more than a system) are insufficient and likely to fail. To reduce this danger, I recommend moving away from the idea of "managing knowledge" when we are actually talking about managing its *flow*.

Some of the pioneers of KM have for quite some time disputed the use of the term *knowledge management*.[7] But for lack of a better alternative and because it is widely used by consultants and "KM software vendors," the term has persisted. It still represents a possible answer to that one big problem that almost all organizations would like to solve: How can I make the best use of the knowledge (present, past, and future) in the heads of the people in my organization?

After a long time of playing with alternative terms, the one that actually fits best with my understanding is *knowledge flow management,* because the thing that you *can* manage is the flow of knowledge. You can speed it up by providing tools and technology as a foundation. You can enable a flow by creating an environment that people find safe, attractive, and efficient and that motivates them to share their knowledge. This could be either face-to-face or by recording relevant information that can be used by others to re-create knowledge in their frame of reference. The flow can be influenced with the help of certain individuals and their actions and behaviors. Chapter 3 discusses the different roles that those individuals will have to play.

The term *knowledge management* will probably stick for a while longer, but if you want to get to the heart of the problem, I advise that you also start using new language. The focus of knowledge flow management is different, and the investments will be different. And as resources are inherently scarce, putting resources into the wrong activities can be a major reason for failure.[8]

TAKING A HOLISTIC VIEW

In 1998 I attended an early KM conference at the Chicago Pier Conference Center. Organized by DCI, the conference was packed with presentations, many of which had the term *knowledge management* in the title. Most of the presentations started with "KM is 80 percent people and 20 percent technology," and then presenters went on to talk 100 percent about technology. But not all followed that pattern. There were a few exceptions, such as a presentation by Etienne Wenger talking about communities of practice that was the big eye-opener for me in discovering what KM is really all about.

The worst of the presentations was a keynote by a high-level Lotus executive that began with "I am not going to talk about technology," only to follow five minutes later with a video that turned out to be a Lotus Notes technology commercial. I went home largely disappointed by the conference in general but exhilarated by Etienne's presentation.

He sparked something in my mind that grew to a major fire over the last decade.

The formula in Chicago was usually:

$$KM = People + Technology$$

And some went as far as extending it to:

$$KM = People + Process + Technology$$

When I was driving the topic within SAS, I found that it made a great target for three-ball juggling. As it happened, I was asked by the organizers of our company sales kick-off meeting if I would dare to put up a little entertainment during that event. My response was "Sure, as long as I can pick any topic I like to talk about while I am doing it." So I created a short juggling routine that was essentially a presentation on KM concepts the way that I understood them. And it all started out with juggling three balls representing the key ingredients: people, process, and technology. It was easy to show visually where things can go wrong. I got great response from the audience, and what made me especially happy was that people remembered more than the tricks. After the show, I was able to dive deeper on the topic with a number of people who approached me, and as a result I definitely increased awareness. A lack of awareness of the importance of sharing knowledge is one of the top barriers, as discussed in Chapter 6.

I repeated the kick-off juggling presentation for several years, with a different focus every time. It was a little bit like a yearly live-blog entry for my colleagues. After a couple of years I added a fourth ball, which represented "culture," as I realized that without the right culture, the other three elements are very hard to bring together.

In the juggling routine, the balls representing the elements are basically all equal in size, but I do point out that the focus needs to be disproportional. Culture and people account for about 70 percent, process 20 percent, and technology 10 percent. One thing to clarify here is that those percentages represent the main effort that goes into the initiative to get it started successfully. Once everything is fully up and running and integrated into your organization, the proportions that those components play may shift. For example, technology might play a bigger role. But when you start out, the emphasis should be on the human side.

Technology is often the easy part, and that is why too often the efforts are focused on it. "We will deal with the other things later" is the common thinking. Chapter 7 discusses this *technology trap* in more detail.

If you want to take only one thing from this book, then let it be the fact that successful knowledge flow management needs a holistic approach and that working on the hard stuff (the people issues) will be your most important task. By *holistic approach* I mean an approach that covers all elements according to their final impact on success. Many people still believe that technology is the biggest portion of that equation. But with many organizations considering that their KM initiatives have failed, it seems clear that the other two probably did not get the attention they deserved.

What do I mean when I talk about focus on people? Especially within the area of knowledge flow management, it is essential that people are fully involved, motivated, and prepared to share high-potential information based on knowledge they built. Otherwise, any initiative that attempts to enable knowledge to flow through the organization will provide only a fraction of the potential value. And to take it to the extreme, every cent invested in technology could be a pure waste of money. Without proper real attention to the other components for success, you might as well invest the money into something more worthwhile. In fact, if you get presented with any proposal for a "KM" initiative that will spend 95 percent on technology and only 5 percent on (ongoing) costs for support functions (and this includes not only technical support, but marketing, training, strategy, etc.), you might as well take the 95 percent sum and donate it to a good cause of your choice.

Within the holistic view, there is another way of looking at humans and technology. It is the degree of automation that you should strive to create. This is where process comes into play. Process is the piece that brings the other two elements together. In my mind, the degree of automation (the human and technology pieces) are two parts on a continuum, the technology–human continuum (see Exhibit 1.1). And the big question is: Where is the cut-off point? How much technology

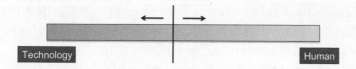

Exhibit 1.1 Technology–Human Continuum

should we have, how much process should be automatically embedded in the technology, and how much do we leave it to people and their ability to create, follow, and adapt processes? The cut-off point moves frequently. With new technologies, the cut-off point moves to the right, but with the greater sophistication of people and increased complexity and expectations, it moves back to the left.

One great example of a movement of the cut-off point back to the left is the way that people share knowledge via some of the social media tools that came with the Web 2.0 wave. Twenty years ago, everybody was talking about technology agents that deliver all the information to us automatically. We would not have to do anything other than turn on our computer and ask some agent any question in natural language. Contrary to the predictions, I do not think many organizations are even getting close to that scenario. The more sophisticated ones have business intelligence technology in place that will automatically highlight key events and trigger automatic pushing of information, but when it comes to a lot of our daily questions in our professional and personal lives, these days people ask their peers, call an expert, or post a question in some social community like Twitter.

Basically they are turning to "human" agents. The big difference is the scale at which we have those human agents at our fingertips these days. Space and time are not really limitations anymore. I can post a question on a Twitter stream and might get responses in minutes from literally any corner of our planet.

Following blogs can also be seen as using a human agent. Instead of scanning the Web for news and tips on photography, I can follow two or three expert photography bloggers. Apart from being experts, they also spend the majority of their professional or personal lives scanning the Web and consolidating, collecting, and positioning what might be relevant to me. As long as I trust those bloggers and the sources they consolidate, this process is a lot more effective than if I tried to spend the time myself.

So instead of taking a "me-central" view of my computer and some electronic agents that go out and try to make sense of the information that is available, by following blogs I am using human agents who each represent an entry point into a larger community. That community practices what I am interested in and represents a body of knowledge on that topic.

This is a great example of an interesting shift in the technology–human continuum. The turn to trusted human agents is also something that plays a major role in communities of practice.[9]

One other reason for using a holistic approach to manage the organizational knowledge flow is what Peter Senge calls system thinking. In his famous book *The Fifth Discipline*, Senge introduces system thinking as the most important discipline that lets you look beyond snapshots or isolated parts of your system.[10] For success, you must look at the different components that make up your knowledge flow and how they influence each other. Concentrating on one of them (i.e., technology) alone will be highly insufficient.

But even under the holistic view, the framework needs to be open and simple. So it is not about prescribing everything to the lowest level with extensive and perfect process descriptions. You should create simple rules that are easy to understand and follow, and within those rules you provide degrees of freedom to get innovative adaptation. The rules themselves need to be followed consistently. But within the boundaries of those rules, groups and individuals have considerable flexibility.

Some powerful examples that follow this successful pattern are:

- **The Toyota Production System.** Individual workers have the freedom in their small groups to change processes very quickly and autonomously, but they operate in a strict framework of conduct, collaboration, and feedback procedures to make sure that successful processes travel to other parts of the organization.[11]

- **The Web.** The basic rules for the Web were simple. The addressing scheme and cross-linking functionality built the basic framework to an unprecedented technological and social revolution that in its global reach has surpassed anything like it before. Within those simple rules, individuals and groups have the possibility to produce any type of content they can think of. Not all of it is desirable or legal, but those are the side effects that a dynamic system is likely to produce that need to be dealt with.

- **Wikipedia.** As a subset of the Web, Wikipedia conquered a large portion of the encyclopedic market based on some simple principles. Anybody, including nontechnical people, can define terms via simple-to-edit Web pages. The set of rules to follow started out extremely simple and needed to be refined and made a bit more sophisticated. But Wikipedia produced a way for the masses to participate by defining any term that comes to their minds, and for many it was their first encounter with Web 2.0.

- **Twitter.** This microblogging service is showing extraordinary growth and makes simplicity the main mantra. Limiting each post to 140 characters forces people to be concise. Twitter offers extremely easy ways to knit networks among truly global participants via that little "Follow" button. The rules are simple, the scaling is large, and the effects are amazing. It appeals to people interested in any imaginable topic, whether it is the exchange of technical information or swimming tips. As with the Web in general, there are certain behaviors, such as spamming, that might create serious challenges to the system, but the community will counter those behaviors if they still see value in the system.

- **The iPhone.** The principle behind the iPhone is a simple, attractive, and appealing interface that provides a framework for a range of applications. The device combines a strong brand and excellent marketing with innovative and appealing technology.

  The actual functionality of the basic device was simple, and users are provided only a handful of applications to start with. But Apple made it very easy to obtain as many additional applications as you like. The key was involving thousands of external developers to create any type of smart or not-so-smart application based on a common set of rules (programming standards). Another key was a platform to easily share and sell them to millions of users. And Apple did not start from scratch, as there were already millions of users of iTunes before the iPhone hit the market. Because iPods had been around for a while, managing media in iTunes is something that many from children to adults is quite familiar with.

As typical prices for the phone applications are only a few dollars, the hurdle to obtain one of them is low, but good ones might well be bought by a million users. This represents the scaling effect that I discuss further in Chapter 5, because understanding this type of pattern can also help with driving your knowledge flow management initiatives.

I want to say a few words on Web 2.0 or what it usually stands for. Some of the technologies and social implications that were introduced by the Web 2.0 era have really helped with the recent comeback of knowledge management, as they represent an easy way to get in personal contact with others to share knowledge. But even in a Web 2.0 or 3.0 or N.0 world, a lot of the principles introduced in the following chapters still hold. This book is specifically not bound to a given technology but touches on the collaboration elements of social media that are great enablers for person-to-person interaction and introduce unprecedented degrees of scaling. Without some guiding principles, some passionate drivership, and some sponsorship, though, social media implementations often do not live up to their potential, especially in organizational settings.

One of the common misconceptions is that successful Web applications are done in a build-it-and-they-will-come fashion, which neglects the very strong elements of strategy and passionate drivership behind them. Without ongoing strategy and care by dedicated (in any sense of the word) supporters, most Web applications would not have been able to reach their current success level.

To acknowledge the growing role that social media and other Web X.0–type technologies play in organizational knowledge flows, Chapter 9 discusses how knowledge flow management applies under those rapidly changing environments.

As many knowledge management projects focus too much on the technology, the holistic view will need to add the nontechnology elements and specifically human and motivational aspects. Chapter 4 discusses human support and drivership components.

GETTING INTO THE FLOW

When I started playing with the notion of knowledge flow, the analogy of knowledge flowing through the organization like a river flowing through its bed seemed to fit for a number of reasons. Flows find their own way, but they can also be guided and stopped by barriers. You can have some individuals steering the direction of the flow on a daily level and others providing the main bed of the river by setting strategic goals for the longer run. Connected to those strategic goals, you need some metrics that will drive initiatives toward reaching those goals. Chapter 8 spends some time on the topics of setting realistic goals, measuring success, and ongoing analytics needed to steer an initiative to success. I also discuss some of the limitations and misconceptions of what can be measured based on my experience.

Even at the start of our KM program, I looked at driving success from two sides: the active side with directed actions and the passive side where you remove barriers that prevent knowledge sharing from happening.

One good early KM study came from the Fraunhofer Institute in Germany.[12] It asked roughly 400 organizations about knowledge management, and one result was a list of the top barriers for KM that people encountered. Removing those blocking stones from the flow of knowledge within an organization often can be more effective than trying to influence people or processes directly.

As knowledge is connected to humans, it is up to them to decide whether they want to share it. Some people actually think that they can *make* them do it, but as David Gurteen pointed out in a video interview,[13] this is a fundamental flaw in thinking about knowledge. And as Chris Riemer discussed in a recent editorial for the *K-Street Directions* newsletter,[14] people generally enjoy passing on what they know, so if they are not sharing, it is mostly because something is hindering them. As a result, managing the flow is just as much about creating conditions that will make sharing more likely as it is about trying to have a direct influence on people.

The good news is that it does not take a rocket scientist to remove some of the barriers, but you will need to know what they are and tackle them with the right approach. In Chapter 6 I discuss the major barriers, position them properly, and suggest some approaches to remove them.

CASE STUDY: TOOLPOOL

At the start of this chapter, I mentioned a specific initiative named ToolPool that I use as the major case study throughout the book to show what a successful knowledge flow initiative might look like. I give some examples and share some stories that should clarify what factors were key to its success. To set the stage, let me quickly introduce ToolPool to you and share some of its history.

When I joined SAS Institute, I worked in a development/consulting combination role at its European headquarters. As part of my position, I worked with a range of consultants locally in the different European offices. One thing that occurred to me while I spent time on various projects at customer sites with my colleagues was a certain degree of overlap in the tools, technologies, and approaches they used. A number of the local consultants were aware of this and had built small repositories of things they could reuse from customer to customer. But the degree to which those reusable assets were shared across the offices was largely based on coincidence. Sometimes I was the one who told people about assets I had seen elsewhere.

So after looking at this for a little while and also finding some of those collections appearing on our growing intranet, I decided to look into ways that we could improve that situation. As I mentioned, there were some collections of tools[15] out there already. One of those collections was a toolbox with a small set of reusable, standardized plug-n-play tools.

Looking at all of this in combination, I ended up with a proposal that I took to senior management. The key points of the proposal were these:

- Tools can range in:
  - Size, from a few lines of text to an application with thousands of lines of programming code.
  - Quality, from a raw concept to a plug-n-play component.
  - Location, from staying local with the author to kept in a central place (pool).

    Instead of choosing to focus on certain types of tools, the recommendation was to cater to all of those but use proper categorization. My leading motto was "Don't discriminate, but categorize," which differed from the idea of a standardized toolbox that focused on plug-n-play tools only.

- An initiative to support the sharing of tools had to:
  - Be available to everybody within the organization in a very simple way (I had our global intranet in mind here) and without additional cost that could inhibit or exclude any local staff.
  - Have a dedicated support person over an extended time frame. I immediately asked for at least one extra person, as I knew it would be tricky for me personally to stick to only that one initiative over time.

There were additional parts to the proposal, but I will hit on those factors in the more general discussions where they apply in later chapters.

I got the go-ahead to implement what I had proposed in May 1997. By July 11, ToolPool, as I named it, was ready to be launched. It started out with a very simple Web application that basically represented a registry with a descriptive Web page per tool that followed a common basic structure of information provided. Between the end of May and July 11, I spent some time building the simple Web interface for that registry. But considerably more time was spent building up a launch collection of entries. On launch day, I had a base of 150 entries, a number of which came from the collections that were out there on the Web and the plug-n-play toolbox. When people came to ToolPool for the first time, there was something to find.

The audience to which I launched ToolPool was mainly some of the consultants who had provided the first tools as well as those on specific e-mail lists. It was actually a comparatively small audience to start with. In August I hired the owning support person, and together we spent considerable time ensuring that there was a constant flow of new tools going in. On average we managed to publish about five to six entries per week in those early days.

We found new tools using several ways. Early on, we contacted consultants who had indicated in a mailing list that they might have candidates. We also actively scanned the intranet for candidates, but more and more, as people got to know ToolPool, we received unsolicited contributions from the field. Download numbers in those first months rose quickly to about 300 to 400. A key element of the application that we built in and constantly adjusted to feedback was an analytics component that would give us some feeling how much usage we had and where it came from, something we extended considerably over the years and that I explain more about in Chapter 8.

Year after year, ToolPool has been growing in a number of ways. Being on our internal Web, it quickly went to global usage. The number and range of contributions increased based on marketing we did to other internal audiences. The download numbers increased over the years and are currently between 75,000 and 80,000 downloads per year (i.e., 6,500/month). SAS employs 11,000 people, of whom I would consider maybe 3,000 to 4,000 employees to be prime candidates for reusing a ToolPool entry.

But what is also important is that ToolPool is regarded as *the* place to go for these types of tools. It is an established brand within the technical community of SAS, which includes field-facing programmers, technical support personal, as well as product developers in our development facilities around the globe.

It has seen and survived organizational restructurings and several major software releases, which also represents the evolution at SAS from primarily providing technologies and tools toward the range of customer solutions offered these days. In some cases ToolPool has been a key factor in being able to make those types of shifts.

SAS reinvests roughly 25 percent of its revenue back into research and development, so there is of course a good breeding ground for technical knowledge. What we did with ToolPool was to ensure that knowledge can flow not only within local organizations but across the whole SAS enterprise, which spans over 400 offices in 60 countries.

ToolPool is not only synonymous for reusing technical components; it also drove other types of knowledge-sharing effects, among them an easier way of identifying those with specific knowledge and also helping some people to be recognized as subject matter experts in the organization.

Certain ToolPool entries turned into small open source communities in themselves connecting those who had a special need and interest in a specific technology or solution. And last but not least, there are numerous examples where ToolPool entries have ended up in a product or at least influenced product development, up to the point that locally developed intellectual property would make up a considerable part of a new solution. In these cases it not only saved development costs but also cut the time to market.

ToolPool continues to be a success story even after almost 13 years in use (at the time of publication). What I learned from it over these years and from other initiatives that I started with the ToolPool lessons in mind served as the basis for my recommendation on how you can raise your organizational knowledge flow to a master level.

Since ToolPool is only one out of several successful initiatives at SAS, in later chapters I introduce other examples, such as our skills management and global resource-sharing initiatives.

Based on the case studies, the remainder of the book shows how it is more successful to drive the flow of knowledge in an organization using a portfolio of methods and with a wider focus that covers a lot more than technology.

NOTES

1. *Knowledge management* is a term I use whenever I am referring to the external and current notion of it. See more in the terminology section later in this chapter.
2. Some of my friends and family can attest to the fact that it is easy to get me started but sometimes hard to stop me when I get into the topic. And it does not matter so much whom I talk to, as many are dealing with problems that are grounded in the fact that knowledge is not flowing the way it should be. Meet me at a party and you have a good chance of getting into some type of discussion regarding sharing knowledge and how it might relate to your environment.
3. Economist Intelligence Study Foresight 2020; see www.eiu.com/site_info.asp ?info_name=eiu_Cisco_Foresight_2020&rf=0

4. Appendix B lists some recommended reading.

5. Larry Prusak made this the topic of a number of his keynotes at the Institute for Knowledge Management. The difference between information and knowledge has also been pointed out by T. D. Wilson, "The Nonsense of KM," *Information Research* 8 (No. 1) (October 2002).

6. Ikujiro Nonaka and Hirotaka Takeuchi, *The Knowledge Creating Company: How Japanese Companies Create the Dynamics of Innovation* (New York: Oxford University Press, 1995), p. 284.

7. See the interview with Larry Prusak and Dave Snowden done by Patrick Lambe, "Is KM Dead?": www.gurteen.com/gurteen/gurteen.nsf/id/km-dead-lambe.

8. In this book I still use the term *knowledge management* for cases where it is strongly related to the history of the field or represents the current common understanding.

9. For more on communities of practice, see the section on nontechnical tools in Chapter 7.

10. Peter Senge, *The Fifth Discipline* (New York: Doubleday, 1990/2006).

11. See more about the Toyota Production system in Jeffrey Liker's book *The Toyota Way* (New York: McGraw-Hill, 2003).

12. Hans-Jörg Bullinger, Kai Woerner, and Juan Prieto, "Wissensmanagement Heute," Fraunhofer Institut für Arbeitswirtschaft und Organisation, Stuttgart, Germany, 1997.

13. See www.gurteen.com/gurteen/gurteen.nsf/id/L004395/.

14. See www.knowledgestreet.com/About_Us/Directions/May_2009_Directions/may _2009_directions.html#StSmarts.

15. I will use the word *tool* in a wider sense here; that is, it can range from a document that describes on how to do something, a small tip, a small piece of programming code, or a reusable component, up to a full application or a small application that automates a process.

CHAPTER 2

Getting Started

Q: How do you eat an elephant?
A: A bite at a time.

—Traditional joke

In this and the next chapter, I discuss the basic components of knowledge flow management. Understanding these additional concepts is a prerequisite for getting started with the right scope in mind. The order in which I discuss these topics is not necessarily prescriptive for the order in which you implement them. What area you might need to focus on most depends on where you are in the life cycle of implementing knowledge flow management in your organization. For somebody who has not started a specific program yet, the concepts discussed in this chapter are the key starting points.

PROJECT VERSUS *INITIATIVE*

A fundamental decision to make before you even get started with any type of knowledge flow management activity is the general way you want to approach it. Often I hear people talking about a "knowledge management project" they are just about to start. You might have noticed that I usually speak of initiatives, not projects. I believe that there is a difference between an initiative and a project.

A project by definition has a beginning and an end. An initiative—the way I define it—could be short or long term, but in general I see it as an ongoing activity that does not necessarily have a predefined end. As long as an initiative provides value, it could go on year after year, potentially with a modified focus and slightly changing objectives.

Certain subactivities under the umbrella of the initiative could be run as projects, though. If you create and install a technical system to support certain parts of your knowledge flow, this is an example of a project within the initiative. But it is only a small piece of the complete initiative, and without the other components, the project by itself provides limited value. So I see a project as an activity with a defined beginning and end that would be run within an initiative. One element projects and initiatives have in common is that they need funding and measures to see whether activities are on track to reach predefined goals.

Ongoing efforts will ensure that the result of a project fits the overall strategy and changing conditions within the initiative. Those efforts and support activities include not only the technical support for the system but, even more important, all those actions to sustain or grow ongoing effective participation. This includes marketing efforts, such as evangelizing to parts of the organization that could benefit but might not even be aware of any potential.

If you talk only about a *project*, the word brings with it the danger that key stakeholders might feel they can finish one specific knowledge management project, then be done with knowledge flow management and take the resources off and use them somewhere else. While talking about a *project* might work for creating and rolling out a technical system by itself, it is a sure recipe for failure when you want to get ongoing value from what you created. One of the key success factors for a successful knowledge flow management initiative is the availability of longer-term passionate resources that will guide it.

Knowledge flow management is largely about driving human behavior, which often takes considerably more time than a pure information technology (IT) project. It might take years rather than months to get an initiative not only launched but also embedded into the organization to the point where it is part of normal business processes.

I refer to this phase as the *bootstrap phase*. Being patient enough to surpass the bootstrap phase can be well worth it, though, as the return on highly leveraged knowledge can be considerable if not a prerequisite for organizational survival.[1]

Having a consistent strategy during the bootstrap phase is a key requirement for success. That does not mean that there should not be any fluctuation in your support team. In fact, it can help to get some fresh ideas, but because the key ideas have to be consistent, a core team should be there longer term. Apart from consistency, you should focus on a manageable number of initiatives to which you can devote full attention for an extended time in order to move from the bootstrap phase to the point where participation in the initiative becomes a standard business process. And even if participation has become a natural element of business operations, the need for support will not diminish completely.

One more reason for closely guiding these initiatives is the potential for innovation. When it comes to the supporting technology, there is a difference between operational systems, such as a typical finance or personnel system, and technology used to support knowledge flow. Operational systems are usually created with extensive phases of requirements gathering, larger phases of development, and rather infrequent update release points. Technical systems created to support knowledge flow management initiatives need to be extremely flexible and agile. For operational systems, it is easier to prescribe standard procedures. You can just demand that everyone in human resources (HR) use the new HR system. In some cases legal compliance rules might mandate usage. When it comes to knowledge sharing—and specifically if you want the most valuable knowledge to flow—you cannot just prescribe participation. It is the knowledge in people's heads that needs to be shared. So it is essential that you make participation in the initiative as attractive as possible and remove any potential barriers. Some of those barriers are discussed in Chapter 6. If you want that behavior to become part of the standard processes, it is important to ensure that the support system and the processes fit together.

In my experiences with ToolPool and other initiatives, this fit can be achieved only via ongoing monitoring of participant behavior. The behavior will likely change over time, and it is important to be aware of that. It is essential to modify systems and processes very quickly should there be any conflict, even if the conflict is based only on some type of fear. People might be afraid to lose some of the value to the organization because they shared their knowledge, for example.

When I talk about a quick reaction, I am thinking of a response within days, not months or years. In the case of ToolPool, we reached out to our users daily—especially during the bootstrap phase—and if we heard that certain things were not working well or not fitting the process, we reacted and adapted the process or system sometimes that same day. If you start with a small user group, you can afford that type of flexibility. With a launch to 10,000 employees, it is a lot more risky.

By starting iteratively, early participants will be more likely to form a positive attitude toward your initiative as they see that it adapts to their wishes almost instantly. It makes them realize how much they are part of the initiative. They can influence how it works, and by the time your initiative grows and reaches additional audiences, you will have fixed some of the major issues and won some additional regional evangelizers.

It is actually easier to accept a slow start than to work with a standard operational system. If only a portion of your organizational knowledge flows more effectively, you are still better off than if you had no flow at all. Another advantage of the staged approach is the potential to collect some specific success stories that can be used to build further support from additional participants and key stake-holders. An example might be a use of some shared knowledge that immediately results in high return.

But the staged approach does not work without a connecting strategy and some passionate support people who can adapt the strategy to changing business requirements. I refer to those passionate support people as *drivers* because they drive the initiatives forward. I also talk about *drivership* as the collective activities of drivers to move a knowledge flow management initiative along.

Make sure to view your knowledge flow management activities longer term and open-ended—not as a fixed-time project. Also ensure that they have that persistent ongoing drivership without too much turnover of your key strategists.

TEAM STRUCTURES

Another important decision to make at the beginning of an initiative is the structure and location of your support team (or perhaps a single driver to start with). There is a range of possibilities:

- You could have a separate knowledge flow management team that oversees your initiatives.

- The drivers could be part of an existing internal service organization, such as the HR, IT, finance, or marketing division.

- It could be part of a standard business function, such as sales or education if there is special need for knowledge flow activities in those areas and if the organization is not ready to have a central knowledge flow management team in any of the internal services organizations.

- You could have a virtual team that has knowledge managers in different parts of the organization with a responsible owner coordinating.

It is important that the key team members have the capabilities and powers to reach outside of the organization in which they are located. In some organizational cultures, this is possible even if the team members sit in one of those mentioned suborganizations. In other cultures, it will be possible only when they are located outside of any of those organizations in a separate entity reporting to the chief executive officer or chief operating officer. The reach across different functions is important, as most initiatives will have a combination of human, technical, and business process elements, and the knowledge flow management team will have to reach out to stakeholders in all of those areas.

A useful structural element is the existence of champions throughout the organization who will drive knowledge flow management initiatives at the local level. In our case, we called them *knowledge coordinators*. They are organized in a global community of practice, but their main focus is the local organization they report into. They are knowledge intermediaries,[2] mediating knowledge flow management processes where necessary. I discuss roles further in Chapter 3.

STRATEGY AND ASSESSMENT

Your knowledge flow management strategy is very much dependent on your organization. Outlining the perfect overall strategy for you is beyond the scope of this book. Your strategy will have to be embedded into the overall company strategy, and your focus will need to support one or more key company objectives. You will need to develop a strategy together with your business stakeholders and in close cooperation with your organizational leadership.

There are, however, some general components that you should cover in your strategy. The framework outlined in Exhibit 2.1 provides some of the main elements that are needed.

Your efforts will be based on the culture of the organization you are dealing with. Your strategy will have a technology foundation that some of the support systems you might build are based on. There will be a set of processes guiding how things get done. Some of those processes might be embedded in systems; others are laid out in documents that are either followed or not. There will also be some processes that are just understood by those following them without being documented. Very often, however, they will represent the way things get done.

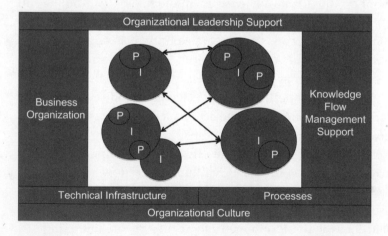

I = initiatives
P = projects

Exhibit 2.1 Knowledge Flow Management Framework

1. Have you planned for and budgeted as much investment in human drivership as you have into technology?

Yes   No

2. Do you have a plan in place as to how you want to sustain or at least manage your knowledge flow management initiative in two, three, and five years? It will likely take multiple years to get your initiative fully established and integrated into processes, an integration that is highly unlikely if you implement inflexible solutions that work now and only now.

Yes   No

3. What are the chances that you will have an ongoing leadership of your initiative? How likely is it that the main evangelizer will have left the organization or be doing something completely different two years from now?

Very likely   Somewhat likely   Will not happen

4. Are key stakeholders looking for a technical product evaluation as one of the first activities? If so, you need to do a lot more work explaining what you are after.

Yes   No

5. Do your key stakeholders mix the words *knowledge* and *information* freely, unaware of any difference? If so, you might be on the way to an information system, but it would not really help with supporting your knowledge flow outside of basic data and information exchange.

Yes   No

6. Do you have top management buy-in? Buy-in does not necessarily mean a big, glorious statement. More important is top management's true belief that knowledge is vital to the organization. They must be willing to take risks and invest even if there is not an immediate payback. A big launch statement without any such belief is not enough for sustainable success. In fact, it actually might be counterproductive as it sets very high expectations for short-term magical solutions.

Full long-term buy-in   Launch and leave buy-in   No buy-in

Exhibit 2.2 Knowledge Flow Management Readiness Questionnaire

7. Have you collected success stories from within your own organization that you can use in the drivership message?

Yes   No

8. In planning technical infrastructure, do you plan to put considerable emphasis on the development of an easy-to-use administrative interface? (The administrative interface will ensure that you will be able to manage contribution quality and a range of user requests with a relatively small group of support staff.)

Yes, I have planned for that   No

9. Will you get buy-in from top management and human resources to invest into developing special roles to support the knowledge flow?

Yes   No

10. Is your main sponsor focused to a large degree on any of the following?

a. Hard measures that prove that the knowledge flow management initiative is providing value within two to three months of its implementation

Yes   No

b. Direct (monetary) rewards for participation (i.e., money for each contribution)

Yes   No

c. Only the "highest-quality knowledge"

Yes   No

d. A central or gatekeeping approach, where all "knowledge" flows through some type of agency that evaluates it

Yes   No

e. A big-bang launch

Yes   No

f. An approach that will ensure coverage of all relevant factors of the current business process to make it very simple and intuitive for the user when the initiative starts (i.e., mirroring a high proportion of current business processes in a system)

Yes   No

Exhibit 2.2 (Continued)

Score your answers using the following key:

1. Yes: 10   No: 1

2. Yes: 10   No: 2

3. Very likely: 1   Not likely: 2   Will not happen: 10

4. Yes: 8   No: 2

5. Yes: 10   No: 2

6. Full long-term buy-in: 10   Launch and leave buy-in: 2   No buy-in: 0

7. Yes: 8   No: 1

8. Yes, I have planned for that: 10   No: 1

9. Yes: 7   No: 2

10.
    a. Yes: 3   No: 8
    b. Yes: 1   No: 1
    c. Yes: 1   No: 8
    d. Yes: 0   No: 10
    e. Yes: 1   No: 8
    f. Yes: 1   No: 8

At the core of your knowledge flow management activities are some initiatives with a longer-term focus. Within the different initiatives you might run certain projects to implement infrastructure, create and run marketing campaigns, or drive processes forward.

The activities are framed on one side by the business organizations, the parts of your organization that participate in the initiatives for the sake of better business results. The support organization drives the initiatives, ensures participation, and guides changes to the underlying platforms (processes, technology, and culture).

The initiatives themselves can actually be viewed as separate entities, but it is important to connect them intelligently. Doing so could include connecting subcomponents, such as technical subsystems. As an example we enhanced our global online staff directory by showing a list of contributions and usage data.

When you develop or refine components for your own organizational strategy to support the knowledge flow, there are a number of factors that you should keep in mind. It is easy to jump to an action plan to implement or enhance certain subcomponents.

I recommend putting any proposal through the following acid test of questions (see Exhibit 2.2)[3] to see if you are really ready to start. These questions are based on experience with a range of initiatives and projects, some successful and a few unsuccessful ones. You can use them for a self-check or to get a better understanding of your key stakeholders motivations and vision. The questions can also be used to uncover areas where the organization is not ready to go forward with their knowledge flow management initiative.

Add up your score and see where you fit:

134–115: You are looking quite good, but if you did not get a perfect score, you should look at the question(s) where you scored low points.

115–100: Risky, but if you can come up with ways to turn around where your answers scored on the low side, you might turn it into a success, after all.

Below 100: You should seriously reconsider if you are really ready to get started. You might be on the road to wasting a lot of money. You probably will need to do a lot more education to get people to understand the real challenges of your knowledge flow.

This questionnaire does not replace a proper complete assessment, of course, but it can highlight some possible danger points early on.

BIG BANG OR SMALL

As I touched on already, there are different approaches to launching initiatives to support your knowledge flow. Let us look at a couple of sample scenarios.

- **Scenario 1.** You gather requirements from the wider organization for the next six months, then spend another six months building a technical system to support the initiative. At the same time, your team is defining all the processes that stake-

holders and participants will have to follow. After the requirements phase, you stay fairly quiet about the initiative. (After
all, you do not want to spoil the great surprise.) You then
launch the initiative and the system that comes with it on day
X as a major breakthrough for the organization with top management announcements and support statements. At that time,
everyone is asked to participate by contributing and using each
other's contributions to the benefit of the organization.

■ **Scenario 2.** You launch a focused initiative with a small group
of early pilot participants. You outline some basic general processes. You build a focused, manageable technical support
system tuned for simplicity and usability. Based on feedback
over a few months, you tune the processes, involved systems,
and incentives toward a state in which you think the majority
of your users is satisfied and gets value from your initiative.
You then extend the audience, starting with targeted marketing
to subject matter experts and management of those groups. You
collect specific success stories and analyze growth and other
trends. You iteratively grow the initiative to encompass your
organization on a wider scale and embed it carefully into standard business processes, adapting every aspect ongoing where
needed. During this phase you get your top management
sponsor to officially endorse the initiative.

If you do not have a lot of established successful initiatives running,
Scenario 2 is the one that is more likely to succeed. This is especially
true when it comes to those initiatives that will include social media
and social networking components.

Apart from starting small with one initiative, I also recommend
starting with focused topics. If there are systems involved, keep them
focused on certain topics and audiences to start with. There are a
number of advantages to this approach:

■ You are reducing complexity in several ways. You can focus
processes on a certain audience.

■ It will also be easier to focus from the support side. People can
more easily identify with those focused initiatives and with
their target audience. That will result in a better sense of ownership, which also drives motivation and passion.

One of the dangers might be that you are taking the feedback from the small starting group and assuming that it will equally apply to a wider audience. This is the reason why you need to be very flexible and adapt with growth.

Within a large initiative that often has a large system component, ownership is usually shared so widely that an individual cannot really see the effect she might be having. Consequently, she will not take the same level of ownership and responsibility. In many cases, ownership is one of the key ingredients in creating the passion that is needed constantly. If there is more focus, supporters will see it as their key responsibility to serve their specific audience as well as possible.

Here are the main advantages of approaching knowledge flow issues with smaller and more focused initiatives:

- Any involved systems will be more modular, so if there are changes to one of the subsystems, it is easier to replace or update them, assuming there are defined interfaces with other parts. For example, you might have an online staff directory system that draws from standard personnel data in order to find subject matter experts. At some point you want to ensure that social platform features also are available with a system like that. You could either add those features to the system itself or create a separate entity that deals with the social networking elements. If they are separate but connected systems, you have more flexibility in rolling out new versions that add new features as requested by your dynamic user community.

- Another advantage of the modular, smaller-steps approach is that you usually get successes earlier, which are essential to build on. Within the more focused activities, you are more likely to find and identify cases of real success. Those can be used to get buy-in for the next iteration. Stories based on those successes can really help to garner wider attention and buy-in.

There are of course a couple of downsides to having separate initiatives and specifically separate technical systems:

- For end users, utilizing more than one system can seem disintegrated.

- There is a risk of duplication of information and efforts in all areas.

In my experience, the best way to deal with these issues is through the creation of *intelligently networked systems*. What I mean by that term is that each module that has a relationship to another module is linked at a touch point, which could be common categorization, for example. These touch points include simple sets of categories (e.g., countries, products, etc.) or more complex taxonomies.

Let us take a simple example from ToolPool: the tools, tips, and tricks sharing initiative. Within the system supporting ToolPool, there is a simple search interface that lets you find entries by keywords. But ToolPool is not the only source of technical content at SAS. Another important resource is the customer problem tracking application. Customer support staff can mark certain problem tracks as tips and tricks instead of software problems. As our partners and customers build and use more complex applications, our customer support not only deals with software problems and errors but also often provides guidance and consulting on how to solve specific challenges. Those customer interactions are tracked but usually will not result in any request for a fix to the software.

The customer tracking process and ToolPool are supported by separate systems, but they are intelligently linked. That means if users do not find the right solution in ToolPool, they will get an easy, one-click way of forwarding their search to the customer tracking center tips and tricks area. However, customer support agents have an easy way to search not only their tracking system but ToolPool as well.

While the systems used are part of different knowledge flow initiatives, a link enables the user to travel from one to the other. At the same time, it is possible to upgrade the tracking system or make changes to ToolPool independently as long as the cross-search linkage stays intact.

It is often an advantage to start with a focused search first and then work into adjacent areas depending on your needs. In this case, we found the concept of modular intelligently networked systems is often a lot more appealing. Actually what we created in the late 1990s is very similar to the approach of using mashup applications in the

Web 2.0 world today. An example for a mashup would be the possibility to link from a real-estate Web site to a map application. The linkage is via address or coordinates. As a starting point, you might see a listing of properties with pictures. Only if you are more interested in a specific property would you move to the actual map application to show the exact location, satellite picture, street views, and more of a property.

Approaching problems of this kind using smaller steps is a common theme, especially in the Web application landscape.[4]

The big picture is an application framework with enough flexibility to plug in a range of smaller components and that obeys a common standard—in programming terms called an API (Application Programming Interface)—that leaves it open as to what type of component somebody might want to build and integrate. The key is that all those small components can be connected intelligently to some degree.

So far in this section I have mainly given examples that have a strong technical component. But you can ask how wide or focused you should be in beginning *any* components of your knowledge flow management efforts.

In the next example, sharing of knowledge happens person to person mostly through side-by-side engagements. The example initiative discussed involves sharing experts throughout the organization in a market model. The basic idea is that those in need of specific subject matter expertise will submit a request for a suitable expert. A brokering service identifies candidates and presents them to the requestor, who then selects a favorite candidate and negotiates details with that person's manager. As a result, the expert will travel to the area of the organization where she is needed. Part of that type of engagement is the involvement of local staff to build up local knowledge for the future.

The initiative is called resource sharing, and over the years it has grown from exchanging experts on a regional level to doing so on a global level. As with the ToolPool initiative, it started quite small. The process actually preceded any type of sophisticated system, and only a few resources per month were shared. This allowed us to refine and rework the involved processes and iteratively create the right support infrastructure and systems, before we rolled it out on a global scale to share resources among all SAS offices worldwide.

To emphasize again, the key to this highly successful initiative that gives SAS a lot of flexibility is the underlying process, not the system that supported that process. If it were not for scaling, we might have been able to run without any technical system (other than e-mail and phone) for a while.

Some modular intelligently connected systems (a skills database to identify candidates on a global scale as well as an application for processing so-called resource requests) were introduced and allowed for higher scaling, finally extending the process to thousands of engagements every year.

What makes this initiative highly successful is the degree of passionate leadership and support behind it, which allowed us to scale it into becoming fully integrated into standard processes. It provides value to several groups at SAS:

- The project managers, who are a lot more flexible in planning resources and can draw from a much wider pool of experts
- The individual experts, who get a chance to build their experience with international engagements and at the same time become more visible with their expertise
- International management, which can use information from a central system to track resource movement, resource shortages, and training needs

The last point shows that any knowledge flow management process needs to be viewed as just another business process and represents a great candidate for measurement and analyzing. Chapter 8 covers this topic in more depth.

NOTES

1. See also Arnoud De Meyer and Ann Vereecke, "How to Optimize Knowledge Sharing in a Factory Network," *McKinsey Quarterly* (September 2009).
2. For more on human knowledge intermediaries, see "Making Connections: The Role of Human Knowledge Intermediaries," *Inside Knowledge* 4, no. 8

(May 2001), online at: www.ikmagazine.com/xq/asp/sid.0/articleid.A80C3BB4-6C30-4855-85F5-C8A7DBC2F89C/eTitle.Making_connections/qx/display.htm

3. Technology can be a great enabler but going too far with mapping business processes in technology can have significant dangers; see Chapter 7.

4. Also refer to the manifesto "The Small Revolution" by Linda Kaplan Thaler and Robin Koval, http://changethis.com/58.02.SmallRevolution

CHAPTER **3**

Roles

The purpose of an organization is to enable
common men to do uncommon things.[1]

—Peter F. Drucker, American educator and writer, 1909–2005

For a successful launch or relaunch of a knowledge flow management initiative, you will need to involve multiple parties. Some will sponsor activities, some will drive the initiatives forward, and last but not least you will want a large number of participants.

The role of a sponsor seems pretty clear at first. Those are the people who sign for infrastructure, project expenses, and support resources, right? I have found that there can be additional sponsors, and they are just as important for ongoing success. I am talking about the type of sponsorship provided by managers at all levels or even the participating individuals themselves.

One of the strongest barriers for being involved in knowledge-sharing activities is not lack of funding but lack of time. So any manager who allows or maybe even encourages team members to get involved in knowledge-sharing activities is a major sponsor. The time team members spend on those activities represents cost but often no immediate payback. In some rare cases, you might be able to embed the activity in a way that it produces quick returns, but that is probably more the exception than the rule. Of course, a strong executive sponsor can have special influence down the management chain.

If managers see the benefit of having their team members attend international community events with potentially substantial travel costs, they are acting as major sponsors to drive global knowledge flow. The same is true when they create processes that will ensure learning from projects and time available for people presenting lessons learned and experiences to their peers. By giving examples and creating the proper culture, they are sponsoring the inflow of contributions and the degree of reuse.

Furthermore, each individual can be seen as a sponsor. Hardly any knowledge worker these days has a completely set daily routine. A typical knowledge worker decides on the things she will be focusing on flexibly during the day. While a basic portfolio of activities is defined in the discussion between knowledge workers and management, it is left to the knowledge workers to set certain priorities within that portfolio. They could focus only on activities that are 100 percent spelled out in bonus or objective plans. Instead, it is common that they go the extra mile and spend time on sharing knowledge with others, whether in the hallway, during a phone conversation, giving a presentation, or preparing some type of asset for reuse. By choosing their priorities to include those types of activities, they are also becoming major sponsors of your knowledge flow management initiative.

In this chapter, as part of the discussions on drivers, we come back to the idea of including some of those sponsoring activities into staff objectives. It is not a trivial task, and it actually can have unexpected and counterproductive results.

The next sections deal with some of the additional roles that I see important in the process of knowledge flow management.

WHO SHOULD INTRODUCE AND DRIVE KNOWLEDGE FLOW MANAGEMENT?

Knowledge flow management is in large part a change management initiative as you want to improve knowledge sharing across your organization, something that will also require change in people's behavior. So, who should take the leading role in getting this type of organizational change implemented? A method that comes to mind is to involve an external consulting organization. An advantage to that approach is the higher level of specific expertise and experience around knowledge flow management that those consultants usually bring with them. Also, external consultants might have it easier to steer around some political and internal structure issues. In comparison to employees they do not carry the same historic burdens with them. They can also bring some validity to the task, confirming, based on prior engagements, that there is real value in improving knowledge flow. But the use of external consultants has a high danger of overshadowing the need for a very strong internal ongoing leadership for an extended time. By using external consultants, the main stakeholders could come to believe that those consultants "will fix it." And the ownership question for the initiative might not be as easy to clarify. For the initiative to survive longer term, it will need a lot more than just some launch and occasional control activities. If the initiative cannot be embedded and driven with internal support, it will not persist. The result very likely will be a limited knowledge management project, not a lasting knowledge flow initiative.

One aspect that plays an important role is the degree to which the person or team driving knowledge flow management is familiar with the cultural aspects of the organization. This applies to anybody from the executive sponsor to support administrators. A deep understanding of the organizational culture is a major challenge for external consultants, who usually lack that type of knowledge. People usually respect knowledge as their biggest asset. If you want to get to some of that knowledge, it is very important to have a full understanding of individual and organizational culture. Developing that deep understanding takes time. It is not something that you can pick up via a few questionnaires in a short time frame. Organizations are complex entities, and it can take years really to understand, across multiple areas, regions, and divisions, how the organization "ticks." What are some of the hidden agendas? Who are key players? Who are the connectors, and who are the gatekeepers who block information? Some of those questions can be answered through careful analysis. Some of the insights surface only to those who have built an extensive network within the organization over a longer time frame.[2] Not all cultures value knowledge sharing. Fears, real or just perceived, about losing power or even losing jobs are barriers to be taken seriously. I discuss barriers and how to deal with them further in Chapter 6.

Over the years, I have met with a number of those driving knowledge flows in their organizations. The majority of them came from within the organization. They might have been in a leadership development role, a technical role, or a human resources function before they were tasked with looking into knowledge management. In some cases—and I would actually include myself in this category—the knowledge function evolved out of a business unit that tried to solve an efficiency problem using methods to increase the leveraging of knowledge.

If companies hire experts to get started, they usually use these experts as an addition to an existing organization. If experienced knowledge management professionals are hired to start from scratch, they usually make it very clear that it takes time to get to measurable results that indicate a change to a better knowledge flow.

In summary, for ongoing success, you will need strong internal expertise and a number of people who have built a certain level of experience. Some of the expertise can be obtained by the internal experts via involvement in external networks, but they will need to get the buy-in from their management to serve in an ongoing knowledge flow management role for an extended time and be able to practice what they learn and extend their expertise. Short-term engagements or switching people frequently will make it hard for expertise to develop. External consultants can help to introduce disruptive and innovative elements needed to overcome barriers that exist in highly change-resistant organizations.

So far I have mainly discussed the drivership role within corporate organizations. But even in noncorporate organizations that might be highly distributed and do not follow traditional structures, a clear drivership is needed. In those types of organizations, drivership is usually part of a governing body or controlling function. Examples for those types of organizations could be professional communities that have often been founded to support leveraging individual or group knowledge on a larger scale. In such environments there is the same need for dedicated support and drivership as there is in corporations.

WHO SHOULD WORRY ABOUT KNOWLEDGE FLOW MANAGEMENT?

If you start with the primarily technical view of knowledge management, it is easy to conclude that this is primarily a topic for technically oriented people or information technology (IT) managers. But whenever I tell people what I do and introduce it as "helping to ensure that knowledge that is available in one part of the organization is used in another," almost everybody can relate to that. If the people I am talking to are from a large organization (private or government), they respond with a statement like "Oh, we need to get better at that in our organization, things get reinvented all the time, we are big and distributed, most people don't even know what others do." But even in a small organization with 10 or 20 people, the reaction is "We definitely could do better at that" or "We have a clear problem with making sure that knowledge gets shared and we are really scared of the effects if one of our few experts leaves."

Even individuals or very small organizations see the potential to benefit by leveraging knowledge. Take the example of a baker. A baker has special recipes that he will very likely not share, but there might be some areas where interacting and sharing knowledge with other bakers (perhaps not with the competitor on the next corner) could very well be beneficial. Think of ways to deal with government health and food processing standards, some technical knowledge on bakery machines, or insights into industry trends. Today, isolation is dangerous. And the life of a baker might have become a little bit more complicated as well. Instead of trying to figure it out all by himself, he could engage in formal or informal (i.e., social networking) organizations that offer real-life or virtual platforms to share some of that knowledge.

Here is one more example. My wife is a physiotherapist. Most of her work involves treating patients with her hands or instructing them to go through specific exercises. The knowledge she accrued over the years is based on study and experience. She studied in a special physiotherapy school, where practicing was a central part of schooling, of course. The experience is what happened everyday for many years. In her mind those things flow together. Hardly any cases are like any others, as every patient is different, especially since my wife follows a school of physiotherapy called orthobionomy, which focuses on looking at the patient in a holistic way. She works in a very small team, so the knowledge flow between the team members is usually via face-to-face contact by discussing cases and questions that might arise or sharing stories during lunch and dinner. Does she need some type of knowledge flow management?

Because the team is rather small and time between patent treatments is short, the exchange of knowledge is somewhat limited. So she quite often uses a Web-based online message board, where experts in her specific field discuss ideas, therapies, and special cases. This could be therapy related or about physiotherapy office procedures and guidelines. The fact that somebody put up this board, is maintaining it, and is passionate about it has all the elements of a successful knowledge flow management initiative. A number of the participants have met in person at trainings and were able to build higher trust levels. So it is not all about the technology—the message board; it is more about the community as a whole.

Apart from this technology-supported community, she is part of an interdisciplinary group consisting of doctors, physiotherapists, and even psychologists who meet regularly to exchange experiences. The interdisciplinary character of the group enables cross-learning and innovation.

I think it is fair to say that almost anybody could benefit from a well-managed knowledge flow. For organizations, the benefits usually would be expressed in terms of increased sales or reduced cost due to the availability of critical knowledge where it is needed. In the physiotherapy example, the benefit might be a better therapy and increased customer satisfaction, making it more likely that patients will choose the same therapist again next time.

In the case of an incorporated organization, usually a specific group of senior management stakeholders should worry about knowledge flow:

- **Head of human resources (HR).** There is no way he can develop the human capital in dynamic times without building on synergy and learning through sharing of knowledge.

- **Head of IT.** Of course IT will play a major role by providing the enabling technologies. Those will range from setting up the right infrastructure platforms (e.g., e-mail and content management systems, social networking platforms, etc.) to implementing very specific systems to support certain knowledge flow management initiatives. IT could also help in providing measures that will be needed to convince management and finance about the value of improving the organizational knowledge flow.[3]

- **Head of finance.** Knowledge as the basis for innovation, and effective performance can represent high financial value. Making best use of existing knowledge, creating new knowledge by ensuring it can flow and be leveraged is a key factor to contain costs. Reinventing the wheel too often and missing opportunities for success can have a substantial effect on the financial health of an organization.

- **Head of internal communications.** In order to create an ongoing marketing stream about your initiatives that reaches your current and potential participants, you need the expertise on how to craft and deliver those messages. Just as evangelizing by knowledge flow management supporters is important, the communications department can be used to build the brand, highlight successes, and make the value clear via stories posted to larger audiences.

- **Head of marketing.** Only a well-working knowledge flow from your customers to the inside of the organization can ensure that the marketing strategy is well tuned for success. But knowledge from the field usually does not magically make it to your strategy and development departments. Direct questions to those dealing with customers will bring to the surface only a portion of the knowledge they really have; a large portion remains in their heads. A well-tuned customer relationship management initiative can bring to light more of that knowledge. Through smart analytics, additional insights can be generated.

However, there is another very important effect in organizations that supports the flow analogy very well. Knowledge is passed on via direct interaction between those working closely together. It could be via joint engagements or stories being told. In an organization where the rate of interaction is high, the knowledge will eventually make its way from the edge of the organization to the inside. It must flow from those facing customers to those who need it within the organization. Here is an example of that type of flow. Imagine a number of small incidents where a field person watches unexpected customer behavior. By themselves, those incidents might not be big enough to be reported. But as time passes, those incidents get turned into small stories floating around, hit other parts of the organization, and eventually flow toward product marketing and development.

One way to increase the level of inflow is to extend the number of staff members who are facing customers, moving from the traditional model of only certain people directly interacting with customers to a model where a large portion of the organization uses any and every possible opportunity to interact with customers directly. At my company we have done so through a flow of national and international user groups with high involvement of staff not only from marketing but from support, consulting, research and development, and, of course, executive leadership from all parts of the organization. In the age of Web 2.0, social media offers an additional way to get involved with many customers more directly.

To increase the flow more generally, offer sufficient possibilities for employees to interact within the organization either in a face-to-face manner or by using social media type of technologies. Face-to-face is still sometimes the only way that certain knowledge flows, but social media technologies can add additional channels that are more cost effective and scale much better. An example at our company is an internal microblogging service that is becoming quite popular as an additional way to connect.

As it is not realistic to rely on a direct flow of knowledge alone, the exploitation of an indirect flow based on increased activity is an important extra component. Organizational culture is a big driver (or inhibitor) of this type of flow. And in this case, it is that part of the culture that lets people interact with one another with trust and respect. Discussing whether you can change organizational culture at all and, if so, how, is beyond this book, but I think culture in today's organizations is still very much influenced top down. Even though collaboration plays an increasing role, for an organization to build a culture, it still needs top management agreement to endorse it first.

I would not say that everybody in an organization should be worrying about knowledge flow management. As knowledge-sharing activities get embedded, it is to be hoped that most of the participants will come to the point where it is just one natural step in the process.

However, there is a need for some people to be dealing with those activities explicitly. Several times I have heard managers issue statements like "We don't need any organization to drive the sharing of knowledge. In our company, it is everybody's job." In some ways, that is the goal knowledge flow management, and in the perfect organization, activities related to knowledge sharing will be embedded to a degree that the scenario just described might actually come close. As far as I can see, however, the majority of organizations are not at that stage just yet, and they will not get to that stage by top management stating that this is where they want them to be or, worse, pretending they are already there. It takes more than a statement. Without that ongoing support organization and a certain number of key stakeholders worrying about knowledge flow management, organizations will not get there automatically. There are too many barriers that need to be addressed actively.

On one hand, organizational leaders state and assert that the knowledge of their people is their biggest asset for being competitive and innovative. On the other hand, organizations seem still not sufficiently ready to acknowledge that specific roles and specific skills might be needed for handling the knowledge flow. Often those tasked with the job are technical experts who will not necessarily have the full range of skills needed for running knowledge flow management initiatives. Chances are they have not been trained in it, or perhaps they expect a silver bullet tool or technology to solve knowledge flow issues for them.

Organizations have realized that it might be a good idea to have an administrator to handle and coordinate certain tasks. Most large organizations do not have every individual make his or her own travel booking without some central support. It is usually cheaper and more efficient to have a professional travel coordinator support the process. There are many such examples where organizations have come to realize that a certain type of specialization might make them more efficient.

So why is it so hard to realize that knowledge flow might get boosts via specialization as well? Let us take an example from a sales organization. Salespeople actually hold a huge amount of highly valuable knowledge about their customers, the competition that they run into, approaches that work and those that do not, typical customer problems, and much more. A common approach to make use of that type of knowledge is to ask salespeople to share their success stories in some fashion or another. I have seen several cases where sales management tried to jump-start this process by offering money for each story shared and written down.

The issue is that a large part of the knowledge is actually proprietary to the salespeople. It is what makes them successful. As there is usually some type of competition between salespeople based on regions, products, and perhaps individual customers, they believe that sharing everything they know might endanger their position.

As a result, a common response is to play it safe and share as little as possible. Another element is time, of course. Even though some think sharing could have a negative impact on their careers, it would not hurt to share perhaps 10 percent of process knowledge, customer issues, and general tips. However, to do so, it would mean that they have to spend some of their precious customer-facing and sales time on analyzing what might be safe and what might be dangerous to share with others. Adding to the issue is the fact that typical salespeople are very good in oral communication but perhaps less good as writers, so asking them to describe sales successes is not really calling on one of their core competencies.

What if you would take a person who is good at writing success stories and have her build a trusted relationship with the salesperson? The writer could use several ways to obtain the basic information: listening to stories the salesperson tells, interviews, or short, very focused questionnaires. The writer would be someone who knows the sales cycle, knows the fears of a typical salesperson regarding sharing, and would be the one to help make the 90 percent proprietary/10 percent safe split. Being sensitive to the issue, the writer would create a sales success story in writing, video interviews, podcasts, or whatever medium seems best. She would appeal to what most salespeople like to do: tell stories. Through listening and transformation, the writer could capture and prepare some assets to be shared. The knowledge represented by those assets might only be a fraction of what the salespeople know, but 10 percent is better than nothing. And the writer would be freeing the salespeople from a task they probably do not really enjoy, they are not good at, and that keeps them from doing what they should be doing: caring about their customers and driving in new sales.

The person just described can be referred to as a knowledge intermediary. The IBM Institute for Knowledge Management (IKM) actually did some extensive research on knowledge intermediaries and identified three major types:[4]

1. **Knowledge brokers.** Mainly concerned with connecting individuals

2. **Knowledge stewards.** Helping others to produce codified assets containing key information based on knowledge

3. **Knowledge researchers.** Servicing others through research and discovery activities of information that is needed to create a certain type of new knowledge

In reality, knowledge intermediaries usually come as some type of hybrids.

In the example of the person who helped the salesperson to identify sharable knowledge and supported the sharing of key information derived from it this support person would be referred to as a knowledge steward. But while the IKM research is almost 10 years old, I have yet to see a single job advertisement for a knowledge intermediary. Most organizations still believe they can make the typical activities that such people perform part of just anybody's job description. I think they are wrong. It is time to think about specialization.

There are actually some educational programs for knowledge managers or other types of knowledge management–related roles now, but often they only cover the MBA type of high-level structuring skills. What about support roles that specialize on a more practical level? Several years ago I spoke at a European conference for HR managers. My keynote was about the relationship between those involved in improving the knowledge flow and the HR organization. I urged those HR managers to get involved in their own organizations, to not let this be an IT-focused topic only. I asked them to think about ways they can drive the development of knowledge-related specialized roles. Judging by a scan through international Web-based job boards, I do not think many have followed that direction yet. You might see a job posting for a knowledge officer here and there or an intranet librarian (with some elements of a knowledge researcher), but we are still far away from having some professions with the necessary focus and expertise. We are still missing experts who could handle the flow of the most important asset that organizations have: the knowledge of their people.

In the next section, we take a closer look at the effects that a knowledge intermediary might have on your knowledge flow.

KNOWLEDGE INTERMEDIARIES

In the late 1990s, we had a problem with people contributing to a couple of our initiatives. As we measured and looked at participation in detail, we found one country specifically to be underrepresented. It was our office in Japan. We saw some participation from the usage side, but contribution numbers were very low based on the size of the office there. In discussions, people told me that was probably linked to a certain element in the culture that makes Japanese people much more careful than those from western cultures in presenting experiences to a wide global audience. Depending on how their contribution is judged, they might lose "face." This fear appears in western culture as well but is especially strong in the Japanese culture. While I did not want to give up based on that estimation, I was not sure how to tackle the issue at the time.

A couple of years later, Japan was number 4 in contributions in the world for one of the initiatives. How did that turnaround happen?

One event that had a major influence in the end was an Asia-Pacific meeting of knowledge coordinators in Singapore. (Knowledge coordinators are those people in our local offices who drive the global initiatives forward and serve as local experts.)

One participant in the group was a young Japanese woman working in our Japan marketing department. She came to our meeting after being in the knowledge coordinator role for only a short time, and she seemed very shy and quiet. Most of the time she left the talking and discussions largely to the more experienced members of the group. What was not so obvious was how extremely thorough and quick her learning was during those two days in Singapore. She really understood the major points of what driving knowledge-sharing behavior is all about, and she went back to her office with a whole pack of innovative ideas. While she did some of the roll-out and motivational activities that all knowledge coordinators were asked to do, she came up with a few activities that were quite specific to her environment:

- She translated the weekly e-mail about newly available contributions into Japanese every Monday morning. It was a great way to increase the number of people who would actually read and digest the e-mail.

- She worked intensively and on a one-on-one basis with contributors, starting with doing a major part of the contribution work, but gradually handing over responsibility to the individuals.

- She offered all potential contributors help to find relevant information and became a trusted advisor, supporting many contributors when they had urgent needs. But she was smart enough not to let people just hand all requests to her. She was also focused on the self-service aspect.

Through those very smart activities, which represented a considerable effort and took a great passion to pull through with an audience that was quite skeptical at the beginning, she built trust not only into her service and in the initiative but, most of all, in the contributors themselves that participation will be safe.

In fact, they discovered that other participants are only "cooking with water" as well.[5] Not all contributors are guru-level experts, but the information shared still could become priceless as it provides a pointer to a person that has just the experiences desperately needed.

The young woman taught us—and she actually presented this topic a year later at a European knowledge coordinator gathering—that cultural translation services might be needed to reach success. She took our strategies and experiences from elsewhere and translated them to Japanese culture. Being Japanese herself, people accepted her advice from a cultural point of view more readily than they would have from anyone in a central driving role (i.e., from headquarters). By taking what she obtained from the global knowledge coordinator community and transferring it to the local Japanese office community, she did just the type of translation that was needed to get her office started.

She did not necessarily fit just one of the IKM knowledge intermediary roles; she was a true hybrid. In helping her local colleagues to get to information, she did researcher activities. As she played an increasing integral role to the local Japanese organization, brokering became one of the benefits she brought to those who used her services. And last but not least, by helping them to contribute information representing their knowledge to an international initiative in a smart and effortless way, she acted as a knowledge steward. People like this woman can be extremely valuable to an organization. Unfortunately, they are in high demand; eventually this woman went on to pursue a career at an international bank.

Typical knowledge intermediaries have extraordinary communication skills and are very good networkers. Through the somewhat general focus of the work, they build extensive internal networks and accrue knowledge in a range of areas. As a result, they are often noticed by line managers as high performers. This then makes them candidates for specialist jobs in marketing, sales, or other parts of the organization.

Those who do well in their knowledge intermediary position enjoy it very much, but another danger is that the intermediary job is not recognized sufficiently. Often management and other key stakeholders do not see and acknowledge the high value of that role right away. They see it purely as an administrative task, neglecting the combination of administrative *and* strategic tasks, the combination of general business knowledge and specialized expertise around knowledge flows. The result could be a rather high turnover.

Unfortunately, the performance of knowledge intermediaries depends a lot on trust and relationships, which need a certain amount of time to develop.

One way to acknowledge the value of people in these roles is to have proper job descriptions and career paths that acknowledge the value of the position. And those career paths have to be linked to value-based payment structures as well.

Good knowledge coordinators:

- Recognize naturally *what* needs to be connected, *who* needs to be connected, and *when* connections need to happen. This is a skill that can develop over time.[6]

- Have the ability to take in a lot of disparate inputs and make sense of those inputs to enable the best possible flow of knowledge to occur

- Are very good at motivating themselves using the stories that they experience everyday

- Show a lot of passion for their job

But even the biggest passion will suffer over time if the effort is not acknowledged. Knowledge intermediary performance is often not easy to measure. Measuring to some degree would be possible but can be very costly. That is, following every project where an intermediary helped to see what her exact contribution was would actually slow down the business process dramatically, similar to micromanaging. Very often, it is a large collection of small effects that make up knowledge intermediaries' value to the organization they support. As the results of improving knowledge flow might lie sometime in the future, it is hard to ascertain exactly what each of those intermediary services was worth.

If people are good at the intermediary job, their roles can become visible to the organization through feedback of peers and internal customers. Frequently, however, the value they provide is more visible to the wider organization than to the immediate manager. And in a lot of cases, their value stays fully hidden because those who make use of an intermediary, for example, do not talk about it; they just keep going to her.

Some possible performance measures for knowledge intermediaries are:

- Feedback from a range of their "customers"
- Indirect measures that evaluate the performance regarding certain strategies that are known to drive positive knowledge flow behavior
- Relative measures that do not concentrate on certain fixed numbers but evaluate organizational changes in behavior or participation growth for knowledge flow initiatives

In general, there is still a large potential in developing knowledge intermediary roles and the framework needed to educate more people to serve in such roles. This is where HR and educational institutions could have an increasing responsibility. As long as the organizational knowledge flow management is not approached with the right focus, not many jobs for this type of role will be offered. And as long as there are no specific jobs for the profile, there are probably not many institutions that will educate specific knowledge intermediaries. It is a typical chicken-and-egg problem. Until the situation changes, it is very likely that you will need to build your own intermediaries internally.

Some of the typical functions that a knowledge intermediary serves actually are handled by certain individuals in your organization already. But it is more of a coincidental filling of the role. In his book *The Tipping Point*[7], Malcolm Gladwell talks about those in an organization or industry who can influence a wide range of others. So you probably already have people in your organization who are natural knowledge intermediaries spending considerable effort making sure that knowledge can flow. They connect those in their network who might profit from sharing knowledge. But leaving it to those special talented, driven people who perform that function often outside of their actual job description is not enough. To get more consistent success, in a lot of cases it will be necessary to have really dedicated and tasked individuals.

The "naturals" are good candidates when you are looking for knowledge intermediary roles to be filled. You might have to deal with the fact that they are usually good at a range of things, and others may resist you moving them out of their current roles into knowledge intermediary roles, where the value might be harder to quantify. If they do a good job in their new roles, they will not only find satisfaction for themselves but also provide a high value to a larger part of the organization. As they are the ones enabling others, having a high-performing individual in that place can have positive ripple effects and the scale of those is often underestimated.

NOTES

1. I am quite sure Peter Drucker meant this quote to be independent of gender.
2. One good tool for identifying key players and networks is social network analysis (SNA). It can help to speed up the discovery process but can also be used for ongoing analysis, as discussed in Chapter 8.
3. See more on measuring in Chapter 8.
4. See more on those roles in J. Sharon, A. Parker, and E. Mosbrooker, "Identifying Key People in Your KM Effort," *KM Review* 3, no. 5 (November-December 2000).
5. This saying is based on the German term "Sie kochen auch nur mit Wasser," which basically means that others are not using any magic; they just use standard ingredients to get results.
6. It is the type of fast judgment that Malcolm Gladwell described in *Blink: The Power of Thinking without Thinking* (New York: Back Bay Books, 2007).
7. Malcolm Gladwell, *The Tipping Point: How Little Things Can Make a Big Difference* (New York: Back Bay Books, 2002).

4

Basic Requirements for Successful Knowledge Flow Management

Nothing of value happens without passion.

—Larry Prusak, 2000, then head of the IBM Institute
for Knowledge Management

PASSIONATE INITIATIVE SUPPORT

In Chapter 3, some of the prerequisites that you will need to get started or revamp your knowledge flow management initiative were discussed. This chapter and the following two chapters look at some new aspects and go into more detail on some areas already mentioned as success factors. Passionate initiative support, motivational drivers, and marketing are ways to get the people in your organization to participate in your initiative and stay with it.

These elements of knowledge flow management are especially important to make an initiative successful for an extended time. The effort to start and especially to embed an initiative into the organization is rather high, so you want it to survive and be around longer term to give you a return on your investment for some time. This does not mean that you should try to keep the initiative alive artificially, but as long as there is a chance it will still provide value, you should do everything to keep going. This type of ongoing survival often is harder to ensure than it is to get it started.

The one key success factor for a knowledge flow management initiative that is above all the others is passionate support. Passion will be the key driver for ongoing value if paired with skills to run those initiatives. It also builds the basis for an initiative to survive the bootstrap phase.

A person can be passionate at doing something stupid or wrong as well, so I would not go as far as saying it is enough to have passion. It has to be paired with competencies, skills, and experiences. As mentioned in the discussion on knowledge intermediaries, this could include some very specific new specialist skills. These skills will not give you full success if they are not combined with some extraordinary drive.

Some years back I tried to explain this factor to a high-level executive; he could relate to it but what he mostly saw in it was ownership. Ownership is definitely a big part of it, but I think it is even more than that.

Merriam-Webster defines *passion* (as it applies here) in these ways:[1]

4. (a) Emotion, the emotions as distinguished from reason; (b) intense, driving, or overmastering feeling or conviction; (c) an outbreak of anger

5. (a) Love; (b) strong liking or desire for or devotion to some activity, object, or concept; (c) sexual desire; (d) an object of desire or deep interest

The type of passion in the relationship to driving a knowledge flow management initiative that I am talking about is the one that is defined under 4 (b) and 5 (b). Key elements are enthusiasm and the desire to make it work no matter what challenges are encountered on the way. Sometimes it means you will have to go to the limit. Some people might even experience this determination as a little too much. It takes extra energy to develop the kind of determination and ongoing self-motivation that is needed for sustainable drivership.

But where does the passion come from? Do you hire or build your passionate drivers? To some degree you will need to hire the right people who have a combination of these skills:

- Extremely good communication skills (i.e., writing and speaking) including storytelling.
- Service mentality (i.e., ready to "get their hands dirty")
- Diverse experiences from multiple fields—not too specialized
- Ability to inspire a passion for knowledge flow management initiatives in others via empathy
- Understanding of what triggers people and how to inspire them to share their knowledge
- Multicultural—preferably has lived in more than one culture for an extended time[2]

However, those skills by themselves will not be enough. Those playing a driver role will have to be capable of building a clear understanding of the value of knowledge; they must believe that for every stream they are creating, the resulting knowledge flow will not only be of value to the organization but can also support their own development and career in the long run.

They will also need to be capable of communicating successfully with executive sponsors, as passion alone will not result in the necessary buy-in and funding.

Apart from getting the right people, you can also build some of the attitude needed to fulfill the driver role. The right leadership is an important factor as well as an ability to inspire some passion in people. There is obviously no way to demand or mandate passion. It is something that develops under certain conditions. You might be able to create some of those conditions to make it more likely that passion develops, but even that is not a guarantee.[3]

As a leader who is responsible for building and sustaining the support team, a lot depends on you and your actions. Some of the methods that can have a positive impact include:

- **Show the progress.** Make it very clear what the effect and outcomes of the initiative are and what part team members play in that process. You can actually make it visible by sharing some of the usage and contribution statistics. While in absolute terms they might not be so interesting, seeing progress is often very motivational to those involved.

- **Celebrate milestones.** Celebrations are important. They represent intermediate success that motivates participants to go for the next level.

- **Share stories.** When you get feedback from the wider organization, make sure that it reaches those involved immediately. In some cases, share it quietly and directly; in other cases, share it with a wider audience so the recognition is more visible. It depends somewhat on the type of person being recognized. Some people really like that moment of fame, but others are embarrassed and are more motivated by quiet and personal recognition.

  Stories are good for more than just recognition. They transport a message that is hard to convey in its complexity in any other form. One good story about a major business success that was made possible with the help of a knowledge flow management initiative can be more powerful than a lot of small synchronous acknowledgments, even though those regular endorsements are very important as well. Besides that, people often remember stories much better than information presented in any other format.

- **Act as a role model.** As a leader, you need to provide a good example when it comes to sharing knowledge. You need to develop and frequently show the value of interacting and sharing rather than hoarding.

Some of these points are important for any type of leadership, of course, but they are especially important if you want to lead those who need to develop a passion for knowledge-related initiatives. They are working in a field where it might be harder for them to prove their value to the organization than if they were in a production or sales role, for example. Trying to get others to share their knowledge takes special effort. A strong leader is needed to show the intermediaries on your team ongoing and repeatedly to what extent they actually help the organization.

One other element that can build passion is identification. Identification starts with ownership, and those driving the initiatives will have to feel that ownership. This is also one of the reasons why smaller focused initiatives work better than very large ones. But identification can also be built using a brand for your initiative.[4]

Using a brand will not only make it easier to sell the initiative to the participants and other stakeholders in your organization, but you also raise the chances that those supporting the initiative will identify with it more closely. By using an appealing brand, you can raise chances that all participants can understand the benefits and relate to the initiative from their day-to-day point of view, which is easier than labeling it a "knowledge flow management initiative."

In Chapter 5 I cover the effects of internal marketing and go more into detail on how you might be able to build a better brand for your initiative.

CULTURE

Qualitative factors like organizational culture and trust between members of the organization can either support a good knowledge flow or inhibit it, as some of the examples in this and the next section show.

Knowledge flows are usually influenced by multiple cultures. In a distributed organization like SAS (with over 400 offices in more than 60 countries), the local culture that people grew up in plays a significant definitive role. This influence of culture could be on a country-by-country basis, but as we also have more and more employees moving around the organization, it is actually a little bit more fine grain. There is a typical culture in Australia, but we might have Dutch, German, or American people working there. How much are they influenced in their behavior and attitude by the culture they grew up in, and how much does the culture they now live in play a role? Depending on the amount of time they have been living in the foreign environment, the influence will be some type of mixture, as I have experienced personally by living as a German citizen in the United States and Switzerland for almost 10 years combined.

Another culture that plays a large role is the organizational culture. SAS is the largest privately held software vendor in the world. Being a private organization with over 11,000 employees and more than $2.3 billion in revenue is unique. The private status has helped over the years to provide an unusually smooth growth curve, with not much diversion from a straight line, even in economic downturns. This consistency has also led to a certain type of attitude and ability to trust one another, something that not every organization might have been able to offer over more than 33 years.

Another element influencing the organizational culture is the business model. SAS has a license model for its software. It starts with a certain first-year fee followed by customers renewing in the following years based on their satisfaction. This model supports a culture where any type of good customer support actually drives a large part of the revenues directly, because if customers are not satisfied, they can cancel the licenses for the next year. The result of this business model is a big focus on ensuring that customers are really happy. For the company culture, it also means that people are more likely to support each other whenever possible. Together with a relatively flat hierarchy and a lot of autonomy for individuals, this is a very good foundation level for building knowledge sharing on top. Of course, like any other organization, there are some people who are less likely to be open for sharing than others, but the standard is considerably higher than elsewhere, as people entering the organization are often surprised to learn.[5]

Admittedly this organizational culture gave us better chances to grow and sustain our knowledge-sharing initiatives over the years. It also made it easier to experiment with different ways of dealing with the initiatives. The principles developed form the underlying framework for the book you are reading now. But you should be careful to not put it all down to organizational culture. Most of those principles work in any type of organizational culture. You might be starting at a somewhat different base level, but the key is to drive constant improvement of your knowledge flow.

Are there ways to change organizational culture? I am not going to dive deeper into change management; there are some excellent books on that topic out there.[6] When it comes to change in knowledge-sharing behavior, a lot of the culture is driven from the top. There is a good example regarding the use of blogs within SAS. In 2007, a few high-level executives considered blogging a waste of time, something they definitely did not want everybody to dive into. By 2009, most top executives in the organization blog internally. More and more of them even have external blogs. By setting these examples and employing new social media tools under some well-defined and carefully constructed guidelines, company culture changed. Gradually more and more people are exploring the effects and benefits of using these media, and a big shift has happened. There are millions of reads on internal SAS blogs every year. The blogs have become a major area of information exchange and lead people to answers or experts. Combined with podcasts and videocasts, blogs are the reason that over 90 percent of global SAS staff feel properly informed about what is going on in the company. What also helped to drive the change process were the stories told either online within the blogs or in traditional ways from person to person.

As this example shows, top management buy-in and leading by example can influence a culture. But it can influence it in both good and bad senses. An example of a behavior that might have a very negative impact would be a manager criticizing somebody on a mailing list. Even if the criticized person might have posted a "stupid" question, there are better ways to handle the situation. Contacting the person directly and finding out what has been driving the behavior is a great way to learn; criticizing a person in the open will kill all the trust of everyone on the mailing list. By carefully educating all stakeholders about the extremely negative effects this type of criticism might have on the general culture, you can remove potential inhibiting factors for a better knowledge flow.

In general, culture can be infectious. As Malcolm Gladwell described in his book *The Tipping Point*,[7] you might be able to change things on a larger scale if you just get over the tipping point. To do so, you will need some key influencers driving a change or have some really compelling events and stories that influence a large enough group. This type of influence is not driven only from the top. Influencers actually could be lower in the organization, but they have an influence on a significant number of others. Sometimes the influencers are visible; sometimes they are somewhat hidden and operate below the surface.

TRUST

The other element that plays a large role and is in some ways connected to culture is trust. Why is trust so important for a good knowledge flow? Because a high level of trust creates a safer environment for knowledge sharing.

There are a number of different types of trust. The two major types that play a role in knowledge flow management are personal trust and trust in another person's skills and knowledge, or topical, trust. While I might not trust a coworker on a personal level, I still might trust in his skills and knowledge. If that is all that is needed, I could still engage with that person and trust his professional judgment. But often personal and topical trust are somewhat related. Most people prefer to work with those they have positive feelings about. As trust is something that usually develops over time, it is more likely that you trust somebody on a topical level if there is at least a certain degree of trust on a personal level.

Trust is one element of interaction that is asymmetric in the sense that it might take years to develop, but a single incident or behavior could destroy it. A lot of the trust that develops between members of an organization is based on the culture and the collection of behaviors that those members experience. Just as an organizational culture is often driven by top management behavior, the same can be said about trust.

Those who share usually open up and offer knowledge that they have built over a long time frame. Likely there are concerns as to what the consequences of them sharing their knowledge would be. The question is "What's in it for me?" It is more likely that people will ask the question if the trust level is low.

If the trust level is high, they will feel that:

■ Sharing their knowledge is safe and will not have negative consequences.

■ There is some reciprocal value for the future or even immediately that they get back for sharing their knowledge.

With a high level of trust, people are not focusing as much on the value question or asking the what's-in-it-for-me question. The situation is almost automatically judged as safe and valuable. This makes a knowledge-sharing situation more effective than if the people sharing feel they have to check whether it is safe to share any bit of knowledge.

However, situations where the sharing of knowledge has led to negative outcomes for the sharer will slow down trust building in the future. One such situation could be being openly criticized for sharing negative experiences, errors, or mishaps. Another situation could be someone using information largely based on another person's knowledge without giving proper credit. This can but might not be an issue for the originator of an idea, though.

For some top organizational performers, this type of reuse of their knowledge by others is not much of an issue. They focus not so much on the knowledge they have but more on the potential knowledge they can build. The fact that their knowledge is reused again and again, helping others will also help them build their network. An additional benefit is that the act of sharing often includes learning as one will need to formulate the ideas in ones head to share them, potentially repeatedly. With these benefits the one sharing can actually move ahead of those the knowledge was shared with.

Trust has that element of reciprocity so usually it is not a one-way street. That means if I invest in people by trusting them and sharing valuable information with them, so they can in turn build knowledge that makes them more successful, I am opening up chances that I will get something back. Basically this creates a feedback loop that will benefit both of us. Feedback loops like these can enhance the overall knowledge flow.

The investment to create those feedback loops often results in positive effects in organizations that generally have a high level of trust, because interaction and sharing become more natural. The investment of time and energy might not return immediate payback but the long-term benefits outweigh the dangers.

Apart from the general culture-driven level of trust, what are ways to increase trust in your organization? Often transparency makes a big difference. If I have a good feeling about the effects of sharing my knowledge, it feels safer than if I see it going into a black box. For this reason, feedback mechanisms are one way to build trust.

As mentioned, personal trust actually can increase topical trust, so one way to raise the general trust level is to create situations where personal trust can develop. Those situations are usually face-to-face ones. With all virtual tools that we have at hand, personal interaction involving all the senses is still the strongest trust builder. In some cases, it can work rather quickly to build a core level of trust that can be built on later.

Here is an example of how trust can develop and support more effective interaction. Some years ago I got a phone call from a manager in our U.S. headquarters. I did not know him, and while he was on the phone I looked him up in our employee directory to see where he fit. He mentioned that there were certain elements where our work might overlap and that he was coming over from the United States to Heidelberg, Germany, the following week and would like to meet me. Not being 100 percent clear on where this might lead, I must admit, my trust level during that call was not really high. A week later, the situation had changed dramatically. We had met, we had long discussions over dinner and lunch, and we had a major project at our hands that would work only with very good alignment across both of our organizations. But what built trust was not so much the project, it was more the level of agreement on certain things, the openness we had developed fairly quickly. Through the following months we were put into high-stress situations and came out of them by focusing on good collaboration. We had frequent virtual interactions but also refreshed the face-to-face trust-building exercises at several meetings.

What I learned from that relationship was that trust has a lot to do with a certain degree of alignment. That does not mean that you have to have the same opinions on everything, but you do need a certain modus operandi on how to deal with situations, an aligned sense of respect. So while a lot of interaction in organizations is moving toward virtual communication, the situation that produces the biggest leaps in trust building are those that involve as many senses as possible, as a lot of the communication in a face-to-face situation is nonverbal. Some example stages (not necessarily perfectly hierarchical) that I would distinguish are:

- An e-mail without prior history is usually at the bottom of the trust pyramid—as it is almost entirely textual.

- A phone call adds another sense to the picture—hearing. In hearing people, you can pick up additional information.

- The next level would be a phone call while looking at the caller's picture. That is why I think a smart phone book that includes employee photographs can be a help in trust building.

- If you add a video stream you get to the next level, as gestures and facial expressions will be adding to the communication experiences.

- At the top of the pyramid is still that personal interaction. It adds touch, smell, true three-dimensional appearance, and more to the picture. Those types of encounters are usually the ones that have higher chances of building trust. Personal meetings even between those who meet irregularly usually involve some type of out-of-work activities, such as dinners and lunches, so the communication experiences will become more complete and the chance that some alignment is happening is a lot higher.

Travel involves cost, so bringing people together on the highest level is not always feasible. An organization has to balance the value that higher trust will produce with the investment that convening certain employees in face-to-face situations brings with it. SAS has had a strong workgroup culture for many years that enabled a good number of those interactions. They are especially good at the start of a project or initiative; thereafter, it is a lot easier to build on that trust level using virtual interaction as long as there are still occasional physical refreshers.

I have one specific recommendation for those running and participating in face-to-face events. Today it is very common to be always-on, always connected. With smart phones and laptops, it is easy to view a day at an international meeting just like one in the office, except that all the daily meetings happen with the same group and you traveled from far away. As there is cost involved in travel, you should make good use of that investment. And that starts by making sure that during meetings, people actually interact and communicate face-to-face. Ask participants if it is really necessary that they spend all their breaks, most of their lunches and evenings running their business back home. Or was the investment to travel high enough that it would be more important to invest in trust building and networking and delegate daily business at home as one might do when going on vacation to the middle of the Sahara? I am not saying that people should not be online during meetings, but personal interaction time should be used for that purpose, not end in groups of folks standing in the break room shouting over one another's phone conversations.

EXECUTIVE SUPPORT

In the section about roles, we discussed the different support roles and how executive support is only one type of sponsorship. In fact, more than just sponsorship is needed. Executive support goes further than that. It actually starts with the insight that the knowledge of people in the organization is essential to success. SAS chief executive officer and president Jim Goodnight repeatedly put it in these words:

> You know, I guess 95 percent of my assets drive out of
> the front gate every evening and it's my job to bring
> them back.

You must fully understand that the knowledge is in people's heads and that you cannot succeed by trying to get it out of their heads and store it in some database. This type of understanding has top executives invest in people and the environment they operate in. In an environment where people feel appreciated and have a high level of trust in one another, it is easier to get knowledge flowing.

Even in economically challenging times, there are ways to provide a better and more trust-enhancing environment than your competition. This high-level support is the framework for certain initiatives to thrive. It is also the trust shown by senior management that will give you the opportunity to test and try out innovative concepts aimed at enhancing the knowledge flow. The same trust that lets SAS invest about 22 percent of its revenue into research and development also exists for initiatives that aim at better leveraging of knowledge. It could be internal training initiatives, efforts to enhance communication, or programs that value field knowledge and field solutions as an important component of the overall development efforts.

This type of executive support does not mean a blind belief in anything that has the "knowledge" label on it. There needs to be a good business case for the investments. With the right executive or general leadership support, it is easier to follow a longer-term strategy and stay in the project portfolio over time instead of an initiative being constantly endangered just because there are no immediate measurable results. In the end, however,, the business case has to prove itself. To be supported ongoing, an initiative must bring back a multiple of the investment.

This point speaks to the type of initiatives that start small and grow iteratively as well. The risk of investment is smaller, and by going about it in a focused way, it is easier to produce visible, real-life positive results.

Apart from the trust in knowledge flow initiatives, executives can undertake a number of more concrete support activities to show their support. Involvement shows their support very strongly. In the ToolPool case, we actually managed to get a top-level executive to send in a technical contribution. It was an extreme example of walking the talk. Another example is the support of our recent social media activities internally and externally through blogging activities. Almost all senior executives are writing internal blogs now. The way they are written, they not only enhance readers' trust with those executives, but they also give a message that spending time on this type of quick knowledge sharing is okay. Combined with the framework given by some well-thought-through social media guidelines, they offer an environment that encourages a growing number of people to share their thoughts, ideas, and knowledge. This could have not developed without a clear drivership from a team of people introducing those technologies with the right processes and the right culture developing around them.

It was an iterative approach. As soon it became clear that the value produced outweighed the risks and costs by far, executive support was not such a hard sell.

Another way of support that is more common with most current knowledge management initiatives is direct endorsement, which often occurs during launch or milestone presentations. An executive stating that she wants full participation from a certain group to solve a business problem, speed up innovation, or reduce reinventing the wheel can send a strong signal that is hard to ignore. One prerequisite is that the executive herself is trusted and respected. In the best case, a longer-term knowledge flow initiative becomes embedded into standard business processes.

The message is supporting the effort, but it will not lead to change if it is not followed up with ongoing drivership by dedicated knowledge flow management team members. The executive message can be used as a reference, but it is only one element out of many. If participants do not believe that sharing knowledge is safe and will somehow help them personally, the executive message will not make a big difference. On the other side, if a team succeeds in convincing people of the value of an initiative and can endorse its message with a clear link to the company strategy and an executive message, the approach becomes well rounded and more complete.

One of the key tasks for the knowledge flow management drivers (and part of a position such as chief knowledge officer) is the ongoing translation and positioning of knowledge flow initiatives in relation to executive messages. How does a certain initiative relate to a strategy put out by the corporate leadership team? How does it support that strategy? How can everybody in the organization involve themselves in an initiative such that their participation will actually help in its execution? Sometimes the relationship might not be clear, or the way the initiative is viewed (perhaps just as some isolated system) does not clearly show a connection. Creating that transparency with all potential participants is just as important as building it with the leadership team, as it will also drive their buy-in and support.

MULTIPLE DRIVERS

Any knowledge flow management initiative needs ongoing drivership, as outlined from different angles already. But it also needs multiple channels for that drivership. Drivers can be people or processes. Channels, in this context, are different attack points that drivers are using to push an initiative forward. This point became very clear in several of our initiatives. When I talk about drivers in this context, I do not talk about people, but more about the motivations or triggers that influence people to participate.

One of the best examples I experienced comes from an employee skills database that we created and that grew to a global system with over 4,000 people registered. When we started that skills database, I discussed my plans with some external knowledge management experts. The most common reaction I got was "Yes, we tried that, it didn't work, the data was very quickly outdated and we couldn't get anybody to update it regularly." I did not let myself get discouraged, though. Our skills database is up and running after eight years, and the data quality is astonishingly good.

What really helped was a portfolio approach of methods and processes created to ensure participation. The skills database is one of the key systems in the resource-sharing initiative that was introduced at the end of Chapter 2. As mentioned, the resource-sharing process is showing value and is accepted and supported on a wide basis. By making it clear that the skills database is an important component of resource sharing, the processes leading to people entering their data got an additional push from local management. Furthermore, those individuals who wanted to ensure that they have a high chance to be placed in interesting projects worldwide made sure their data were in the database and were as accurate as possible. So the resource sharing process was a key driver for the skills database.

Another key driver was the process of skills review attached to annual or semiannual reviews. The skills database as a key planning and communication instrument between employees and their managers drove the motivation. During training and personal development planning, the skills review turned out to be something that many people are very interested in.

There were also a couple of drivers that were linked to measures. Especially in the early phases, we drove some participation by adding a measure to managers' bonus plans: one of the quality indicators they were scored on was the degree of participation in their teams. It was specifically a team and not an individual measure for those entering their data. For some managers, this was a motivator; for others, the portion of their bonus that depended on their teams' participation was not enough for this area to take priority over other factors. But we also made performance transparent to local leaders on a comparison level (portion of team members updating their skills regularly). This sort of transparency can be a good driver as it introduces a certain level of competitiveness.

One driver actually came from a different department. The professional development teams (human resources and staff development teams) started to realize that they could use consolidated data to perform some training needs analysis on a practice level.

So instead of a single driver to push participation, there was and still is a whole range of them. You could see it as a portfolio of driving forces. Not everybody is influenced by the same driver. Some managers do not care about the relatively small bonus component, some people do not want to be involved in resource sharing, and some people are not highly interested in additional training or personal development. But the key is that if you take the overlap of drivers, the resulting set is quite large. And as that set of people participating grows toward 100 percent, you suddenly get another driver: peer pressure.

This description is a good example of multiple drivers, but I think the portfolio approach can and should be applied to any knowledge flow management initiative. You can combine drivers that are focusing on a local level with those that offer a global benefit. And as you are dealing with people, you will always have different types of people who are motivated by different things. Do not be deceived in thinking that just because you are dealing with only a certain job category (just developers, just salespeople, just lawyers), all of them can be herded into the initiative with the same driver. It is much more effective to grow the reach by simultaneously attacking on multiple fronts. The idea is to create enough coverage using different,

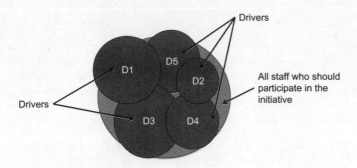

Exhibit 4.1 Motivational Drivers

potentially overlapping drivers to reach a considerable portion of your target audience, as shown in Exhibit 4.1.

It might be hard to find drivers for everyone, and that is fine as well. I am not proposing that a knowledge flow management initiative can be a success only if it reaches 100 percent of your target audience. But you have to strive to get a critical mass of those who are bringing high value to the initiative. Target them first and select the drivers that will get a good coverage with them. The skeptics sometimes join silently, once a high majority of their peers have joined. And their peers could be the ones doing the evangelizing one on one much better than you might be able to from a central point of view.

Another reason for having multiple drivers is the creation of a safety net for changing conditions, something that is actually likely to happen. If you are building and relying on a single driver, and it breaks away, you might need too much time to build up another one. In the meantime, you could lose a critical portion of your audience and endanger the whole initiative. A good example might be the measures in bonus plans. The organization might shift focus, and the bonus plan component related to the knowledge flow management initiative could get pushed out or down to a level that gets less attention. If you have multiple drivers, the remaining ones can catch some of those participants who would otherwise fall out of the net. Of course, it also helps if you have already embedded the initiative into the organization when those types of changes happen. Multiple drivers can make it more likely that this type of integration happens faster. Therefore, they further reduce the overall risk of an initiative failing.

NOTES

1. See www.merriam-webster.com/dictionary/passion
2. Those people who have gone through the process of adapting to multiple cultures and have most of the other skills mentioned here develop an increased sense of understanding for different behaviors. This will help them in dealing with the different types of participants in the knowledge flow.
3. I once experienced a presentation by a motivational speaker who was trying to motivate people to be more passionate about their job by telling them to be more passionate. People felt that they were not being taken seriously as responsible employees; if the presentation had any effect, it was more negative than positive. Using an external speaker in this case made it even worse.
4. When I came up with the name for ToolPool, it was somewhat in contrast to an already existing Toolbox. The word *box*, for me, symbolizes something that is closed, and my goal was to create a large pool of tools that would have a global inflow and represent that area that others could go in and fish from. Coming up with that brand and even a logo was an important element of the proposal that I created to sell the idea to management.
5. See "Working the Good Life" on CBS *60 Minutes*: www.cbsnews.com/stories/2003/04/18/60minutes/main550102.shtml
6. One quite pragmatic recent book is Robert C. Thames and Douglas W. Webster, *Chasing Change: Building Organizational Capacity in a Turbulent Environment* (Hoboken, NJ: John Wiley & Sons, 2008).
7. Malcolm Gladwell, *The Tipping Point: How Little Things Can Make a Big Difference* (New York: Back Bay Books, 2002).

CHAPTER 5

Driving for Success

A wealth of information creates a poverty of attention.

—Herb Simon, 1971, American psychologist[1]

INTERNAL MARKETING: THE MYTH OF BUILD IT AND THEY WILL COME

Any organization that wants to create awareness of its products will turn to marketing strategies to get attention from its customers. Sometimes the same organization will even talk about internal customers for certain types of endeavors. But when it comes to internal marketing, the position often seems to be: "Well, we just order things to happen!" Those having to drive internal initiatives forward often wonder why they have to go through bells and whistles to convince their own staff, get their attention, and carefully nudge them into certain behaviors.

In the past, you might have been able to order that some processes be followed, but with the complexity of today's organizations, the many choices that knowledge workers have to focus and spend their energy on getting people to really change by just ordering them to is not as common. So you will have to apply similar strategies for your internal markets than you do for your external ones. The key message is: Do not be shy about internal marketing.

This is especially true with a knowledge flow management initiative. You are trying to engage people and want them to share something—their knowledge—that they might consider their most valuable asset. How can you use marketing techniques to make that happen?

There are a number of lessons we learned over the years that clearly show what marketing principles might work in this scenario.

Giving your initiative a clear brand is important. When we started out with ToolPool, we actually had an internal designer create a logo. The result was the word in a wave style, both words connected and letters T and P capitalized. We still use that logo in presentations, on internal Web sites, and for a pin that we gave out to contributors.

The ToolPool pin was an idea that came out of one of our team meetings. We were thinking about ways to reward contributors for their effort; the decision was to produce a little pin that they could wear to indicate that they are ToolPool contributors. The pins are little wavy flags with "ToolPool Contributor" written on them.

To this day we are still sending those pins to all new contributors in the company. It comes with a certificate that thanks them for their efforts and for helping organizational success by sharing their knowledge for the benefit of others. That certificate has the ToolPool logo on it and is signed by the chief knowledge officer (who happens to be me at the moment).

Contributors only receive one pin, and that is for their first contribution. It is more about becoming part of a club than getting payment for what they did. The effect of the pin differs. Some have sent thank-you e-mails after receiving them. In a couple of cases where a pin needle broke during shipment, people have asked for a replacement. Some people put them up on their boards in the office. Some probably ignored them and even threw them away. But most staff members are aware that you cannot get one without contributing. Out of the about 1,600 pins that we have given away so far, only two were given away without a ToolPool contribution. Those two pins went to the two major executives who supported ToolPool early on. They received pins as a sign of appreciation for sticking with us through the bootstrap phase.

In some offices, we send batches of pins to a manager of a group of contributors and have the manager distribute the pins during an event.

To be honest, at the beginning, we thought of the pins as just a little sign of appreciation, and to a number of people, that is probably all they are. But one story showed us how different cultures react differently and how the pins might mean much more for at least a certain portion of our contributors.

As there were a number of contributors in our office in Pune, India, we made up a package to send to the manager of the consulting team with certificates and pins. Unfortunately, the Indian tax authorities had an issue with our package, and it got stuck in customs for a couple of weeks. As we had announced the shipment to the Indian manager, he was expecting them and sent us a pretty demanding message asking "Where are our badges?"

The word *badges* really surprised me. I was amazed at how important those pins had become to at least some of our current and potential contributors.

The cost of this activity is actually quite low, only pennies per pin, and as we usually send them via interoffice mail, even the shipping costs are minimal. The effect has been astonishing. It has helped to build the internal brand and was another tool in the portfolio to raise awareness of ToolPool. And it has given a small but personal moment of appreciation to more than a thousand contributors around the globe.

An activity like this will not reach all of those targeted; even if it reaches and encourages only a certain portion of the target, it is worth it, as it helps drive the momentum. Even external marketing campaigns only reach portions of their targets audience.

Apart from the ToolPool pins, there are some other marketing activities that we use repeatedly. One is the celebration of milestones. For this type of marketing activity, it is important to have good statistics about your initiative. In the ToolPool case, two very simple statistics are usage and contribution numbers. We have daily reports on those, and because we can anticipate certain milestones, we are able to prepare events beforehand. Typical marks that we celebrated are:

Tools: 500, 1,000, 2,000

Downloads: 10,000, 25,000, 10,0000 ... 500,000 (We just passed the 700,000th download!)

We also celebrate yearly ToolPool birthdays with special activities. For the tenth anniversary, we were able to get SAS president and chief executive officer Jim Goodnight to contribute a SAS program that he had personally written.

We use those occasions to give away some prizes and create global internal news articles appearing on our intranet homepage. In some cases, we even organized local celebrations.

When these marketing events happen, we usually open up new audiences for participation. At one of those occasions, we actually were contacted by the SAS patent department for the first time. It wanted to collaborate with the ToolPool team to identify patent candidates in ToolPool.

Even though turnover at SAS is very low (below 5 percent), there is some turnover and growth, of course. The marketing activities are also a great way to get extra visibility with those newcomers. Often people get informed about ToolPool either as part of the official induction or as part of the set of standard resources that new technical people are introduced to by colleagues or managers.

Apart from the special events, we also spend a considerable amount of effort on marketing to specific communities within the company. For example, we subscribe to the major technical newsgroups or mailing lists and scan them for contribution candidates. For example, say a consultant asks a question or requests a certain functionality outside of the scope of the current product. Often another consultant has a solution and sends it or a tool as a reply to the mailing list. In the early phase of ToolPool, we would go in and work with the author to turn the reply into a contribution. The author in that case would hardly have to do anything. We then posted back the new location in ToolPool to everybody. While people might not remember the exact link, more and more they became aware that ToolPool was where to look for this and other tools. It frees them from scanning old unstructured mailing list archives, something that is not usually very effective. Having documentation and describing parameters adds value and makes tools much easier to find.

You could tell that the community had accepted the new place to locate tools and authors when people were pointing to specific ToolPool entries without stating what and where it is, and no one asked what and where ToolPool was. At this point, the team and I were convinced we had created a real winner.

Another way to hit the major communities was at technical workshops or international training events. We usually reserved short spots on the agenda, where one of our team members would introduce ToolPool and other relevant initiatives, inviting people to contribute. In some cases this was very fitting as people presented some of their recent tools during the workgroup. Offering the technical community a known and well-supported place for those entities fulfilled an immediate need since people wanted to get easy access to anything shared during the event.

Another way to market your initiative even in a large organization is through personal efforts, as the next story shows.

One Sunday afternoon I was browsing our internal web and found a page where somebody had listed a number of mailing lists. Each list had a link next to its name. I tried one of them, expecting to get an archive of e-mails posted to that list. But instead it was actually a link that opened my e-mail program and created an empty e-mail. I did not intend to post to the list, so I wanted to kill the window. Not fully concentrating, I accidentally hit the Send button. Oh no, I had just sent an empty e-mail without any subject to all the global members of that mailing list. While I was playing with ideas on how to save the situation, the first reply already came in. One of the subscribers replied with a question: "What is this e-mail trying to tell us?" I looked at my options:

- Ignore the whole thing and just move on—but it almost looked as if it was too late to ignore.

- Recall the e-mail, which usually does not work very well, and often makes sure that people *will* try to read it. When somebody recalls an e-mail, it just urges me to find out what the reason might be, and there is often a way to still read it.

- Reply with the typical widely hated response of sending another useless e-mail apologizing for the mistake.

None of these seemed particularly smart. So I tried something new:

I did reply, but the reply e-mail started with:

> While I have your attention now, let me introduce you
> to the following Knowledge Management Initiatives that
> you might or might not be familiar with.

The rest of that e-mail very quickly introduced and pointed to two of our major initiatives that the audience could get value from. (I was fairly confident of this because I knew their topic and focus.) There was not a single additional funny reply, but from system stats, I could see that it produced a number of click-throughs to the initiative support systems.

Of course this will only work once, but it did work that Sunday afternoon. The moral of the story is: As a driver, you should always consider ways to market and build your initiative brand. In this case, I was actually able to turn an error into an opportunity.

The key factor of marketing activities is that they produce regular attention. One of the mistakes I have witnessed is a big-bang marketing launch of an initiative not followed with an ongoing, long-standing follow-up. I wonder how many portals in the world have been launched with high hopes, great messages, and all the senior management support, and then the expectation was that everybody paid attention and, based on that launch message, happily shared their knowledge ever after. But only when they see ongoing value over time will people really put in the effort that is needed. So a lot of those highly acclaimed systems went down shortly after the smoke had cleared because the team launching it was moving on to the next "project."

It is also important for your marketing message to appeal to the issues that people face. Often the marketing of initiatives tries to appeal to their global value. And in the end, the global value will provide the highest value. But that does not have to be the message that you are leading with. You can equally appeal to local value and global value will be the by-product. In the case of ToolPool, one country had initiated a local effort for sharing tools. It even appointed a "tools manager." This was a position where people would take turns managing a local collection of tools. The country had several separate offices, and recognized that just between different locations, people sometimes were not aware of those tools that others had created. As a result, there was reinventing even at that level. But it turned out that they had some challenges sustaining the effort. The round-robin of the tools manager did not really work. In the end, one person did the job for a while, finding it harder and harder to concentrate on this nonprofit extra task.

We marketed ToolPool to that team by saying:

- We provide you with the support end to end.
- We provide a stable infrastructure.
- What you will have to do is provide those tools according to a set of standards (i.e., basic documentation in English).

That was how we channeled their efforts into the global community. The English documentation was actually a little bit of a hurdle, but the value of not having to invest in local resources and still be able to share within that local organization was considered high enough for management to switch and endorse this way of operation. Even looking at it only from their local country perspective, they saw the value they got out of it. In the end, the global initiative was the real winner, with some of the tools that those local consultants provided becoming huge successes in many other countries.

Another tip on how to market your initiatives, at least in the early phase, is to make it hard and easy at the same time. Take, for example, the case of announcing a certain initiative or a system within it as a reply to a posted question on a mailing list. Of course, you want to make it easy to get an answer on a question people might have. But sometimes it is smarter to make it just a little bit harder. Instead of sending out a link to the final content, you could link to the system with very simple instructions to get to the content. Something like: "There is an excellent tool in ToolPool that will do exactly what you need. Go to ToolPool (LINK) and search with keywords KEY1 and KEY2."

You would *not* send the answer directly to the person who asked but answer to the list. The reason for this is that others might have had the same problem, or they might at least have started to think about a solution. If you give a link to the final answer, people will download that piece of content and be happy for the moment. That might be the way to go, if you succeeded already in making the initiative widely known. But if you are still in the bootstrap phase, making it a little harder will give a lot of people the experience of what success in using it will look like. They will have seen it, searched, and found something; you will have gone the extra step of building your brand. And over time, people will know how to feed themselves and actually use the initiative system right away, and leave the list to the most important questions or those that are not covered yet.

It is also important to stay consistent in the way you lead users to your initiative. It is an internal brand. Once you are successful, other areas of your organization will be pointing to the initiative (or parts of it). Make sure they do so in a consistent, brand-building manner, and not with everyone coming up with their own ways to refer and point to the initiative. It is pure (internal) brand building, and I am sure there are other marketing methods you can apply. Talk to your marketing experts.

In the story about the mailing list blooper, one of the key factors was attention. Especially in times when people have many heavily loaded channels to choose from and are bombarded with information and requests, it is important to get their attention. Tom Davenport and John Beck covered the importance of attention in their book *The Attention Economy*.[2] The fact is that without getting some attention first, it will be hard to get action. Of course, you will be competing with other initiatives trying to get people's attention.

Some of the major ways of getting the needed attention include:

- **Use existing channels.** By using existing channels, it is easier to reach people where they are looking. It is also easier to ensure that your initiative gets integrated into existing business processes. The downside is that those channels can be fairly loaded already and competition for attention is high.

- **Create additional, new channels.** Sometimes to get wide attention, especially if you want to leave it more open as to what audiences you are drawing into your initiative, you might want to try a totally new channel or slightly modify a traditional channel. If it is unusual enough, it can draw people in, especially those interested in new things. A good example would be the juggling presentations mentioned in an earlier chapter. The channel—a juggling performance—is unusual. And as it was part of an event that the key players attended for other reasons, it opened up the opportunity for getting attention. A standard slide presentation could not have created the level of attention needed to really drive a few key messages home. The key is to be innovative. Another great example of getting attention in an unusual way is sign spinners. This supposedly started out in California a few years ago, where a few of those tasked with holding up advertising signs at street corners got bored and started flipping them around. Nowadays some have really perfected the flipping and have become street artists who perform sophisticated routines with the signs. The spinning is just the extra touch that makes it appealing to otherwise bored drivers and grabs their attention. So maybe your initiative needs some sign spinners in the organization.

It is very important to understand that individual events that create some attention will not create lasting success. Failure to recognize this is a key mistake. It does not matter how smart your marketing activity might be; if it is a one-off, it will not provide lasting success. It needs repetition for as long as you want your initiative to be successful. It needs a pulse.

THE PULSE

A topic that is related to marketing is what I refer to as "creating a pulse." If you look at your initiative as a living entity, the pulse is what keeps it alive. It is not enough to blow huge amounts of blood into it at the start. Only the existence of a pulse makes it survive. Elements that can help create a pulse are regular events and news items.

One key pulse element that we added almost from the start of our initiative was a weekly e-mail to a list of subscribers. This list was by subscription only. We did not force anybody to subscribe. Nevertheless, today there are about 1,600 subscribers. An e-mail goes out every Sunday and is read by most subscribers on Monday.

To make writing this e-mail really easy, it is partly automatically produced, but to give it a personal touch, it also contains a manual element. With the help of a simple Web interface, a ToolPool administrator adds a short block of text that shows up at the top of the e-mail. There is a template text that the administrator can start from. The text usually has interesting tips, recent news on ToolPool, or highlights specific contributions or achievements. It might point to the first Brazilian contribution or talk about the system being down for three hours next weekend. It might announce one of the milestones or ask for specific feedback or help with an entry. The key is that it is specific to that week; people can see that a human has produced it and is personally turning to them.

The rest of the e-mail is the automatic part and is a manageable, professional-looking list of new entries with direct links to documentation and downloads, information about the author, the contributing office, and more. It also contains ways to get to a discussion list, the main application page, and how to reach the administrators. As there are somewhere between 8 to 15 new ToolPool entries in an average week, the e-mail is not long. Early on, some people asked if we could introduce some subsetting, and we played with that idea. But it turned out to be overkill. One of the side effects of showing everybody the full list is unanticipated learning as people get to see not only what they *think* is relevant for them. They might be triggered by keywords to look at details of tools they might have otherwise filtered out. The result is sometimes an interesting cross-fertilization and innovation.

A number of our subscribers, especially some of the consulting and development managers, have told me that the ToolPool e-mail is *the* e-mail that they definitely read on Monday morning. And in the rare cases when technical problems delayed the e-mail, several people asked what might be wrong.

E-mail is only one way to create a pulse. Other methods we have used were short regular Web presentations highlighting certain content or features. And recently links to the weekly e-mails (which are stored in an easily Web-accessible archive) are being posted on our SAS internal Twitter stream to reach additional audiences.

I believe a pulse is something that every knowledge flow management initiative needs. And as you do not want to overdo it, it is important to have a smart ongoing campaign management that monitors how those activities are received and reacts on feedback instantly. How you create that pulse depends on the initiative. The key is regularity, a good fit to the needs of those you want to get involved, and the flexibility to adapt very quickly.

KEEP IT SIMPLE

Often there is an urge to create a system within an initiative that supports the current business process as exactly as possible. One danger of that approach is increasing complexity and inflexibility.

When I started an initiative for exchanging project experiences and gathered feedback on an early prototype of an application that I wanted to use, a few people wanted me to add very specific describing parameters as fields. But I had seen what happened to an earlier initiative of a reference tracking system. People were asked to provide a large number of parameters; as a result, many were left empty or filled inconsistently. The argument was: "Those are all important and people will *have* to know them." But the reality was that contributors did not take the time to fill them in. The system's data quality was really low as a result. It is very important to start simple and small. Once you have buy-in and believers in the value, you might be able to raise the bar and ask for additional information.

Another issue arises when you try to map a system perfectly to a current business process. Almost always this means underestimating the dynamics of those processes. In the best case, what you offer the users will fit the minute you launch it (and even that is unlikely). But what about three months from launch time: Will it still fit? If it does not, the acceptance rate will go down, and all the effort you put into the system might end in diminishing participation. Remember, you cannot make people go and share their knowledge. If you want to get a good return of investment, it is best to be considerate, leave enough freedom to adapt. Spend your efforts in driving the processes around a system and how you can enable people to use it instead of focusing on a perfect map for a snapshot in time.

This is another reason why nontechnical elements of a knowledge flow initiative are so important. They might actually be easier to adapt.

You can change your processes to align with what people really do, but often it is harder to change a system that was designed to support a process on a very detailed level.

In using this simpler approach, you might have to fight the urge to follow just any requirement that comes up and also work very carefully at objection handling in the launch and roll-out phases. You will definitely have people who see simplicity as a deficiency. Those are the ones who need a lot of hand-holding. My advice is not to focus on requirements coming in through those types of people. Instead, focus on participants who are more comfortable with changing environments, the more experienced ones who will make it work. This should be the role model of future employees. I do not think you should set the bar based on those who are incapable of dealing with change.

For the future, you need those who not only have a lot of knowledge but are flexible enough to rebuild that base constantly. Having knowledge and relying on it as a status quo will become of less importance in a world where the shelf life of things people need to know is decreasing at incredible speed.

Keeping it simple not only means you are going to get your initiative quicker to market and it will be able to survive longer without being viewed as outdated and supporting old processes; it will also attract and support the right type of people in your organization.

As much as I am in favor of user acceptance, in some cases you might have to overrule requests for too much detail. It is a fine line sometimes, but getting this right is another key success factor.

GO GLOBAL: THE POWER OF SCALING

In the end, the focus of my initiatives has always been global. They might start out on a local level, but very soon I tried to get to global participation, because with the scale of reuse, the return on investment increases as well. This is a factor that is constantly underestimated by contributors and some stakeholders as well. The big value in sharing knowledge comes with scale.

Let us say you have an asset (in our example, it is a reusable piece of software—a tool). If someone creates something like that and reuses it himself, the *reuse factor* is maybe 3 or 4. Now, if he shares that tool with one of his colleagues, it might get up to 7 or 8; if he shares it with the majority of his department, it might get up to 12 to 15. But those numbers are dwarfed by a reuse in a global organization with 1,600 consultants in 60 countries. The level of reuse can easily get to 300 to 500.

At SAS, we have tools that got reused over a 1,000 times. To sit down to produce documentation for a tool might take one to two hours, even less in a lot of cases.

If a tool is now reused three or four times and you save maybe an hour per reuse, it might just be worth it. But at a reuse factor of 1,000, the invested two hours are nothing compared to the value it produces. And we are not even talking about standardizing approaches, cross learning, connection building, and all the rest of the benefits.

In a globalized organization (pretty much any big organization these days), it is important to focus on that global reuse element as it might provide high returns. What is also often underestimated, especially by contributors themselves, is the applicability of their knowledge. Most contributors think that their challenges are unique, but in a globalized world, this is often not true. A bank looking for a specific solution in Japan will not be so dramatically different from a bank looking for a solution in Spain. But we all like to think that what we have at hand is globally unique, and there is no way someone else might suffer a similar "bad" issue.

One good way of getting people beyond that thinking is transparency, as I discuss in Chapter 8 when it comes to presenting contributors with the right measures for their own analysis.

So my recommendation is to go for a simpler but global approach and not an overloaded and local one, if you need to focus your resources.

If you think about it, this is also the power behind the Internet hype. Why did all those Web 2.0 applications succeed? Because they went narrow (i.e., simple) and global, instead of going for a high feature set and staying on a local level.

This is what I call the power of scaling. Many business models on the net are based on the principle of providing a simple, cheap application that is built for a large audience. If you can motivate 1 million people to use a free version of an application, you might have enough fans to motivate 5 to 10 percent of those to go for a *high-end* version of it. They will actually pay for an advanced version or services around it. Even spam is based on that principle. Spammers do not have a big issue with the fact that 99.99 percent of their messages get killed by some spam filter. At 300 million messages, 0.01 percent of recipients stupid or desperate enough actually to buy something is still 30,000 customers.

MOTIVATION

Motivation is a tricky topic, and I will not go into a psychological discussion of what motivation is and how it works in general. Nevertheless, the question "How can I motivate my people to share their knowledge?" is probably one that everyone who trying to push a knowledge flow management initiative is asking.

It is hard to really motivate someone directly. It is more a matter of encouraging people to develop the kind of self-motivating factors that drives them individually.

The most successful approach is through a portfolio of methods to enable this *self-motivation* to develop. Any organization will have a range of people who are driven by different things. Some people are driven by acknowledgement. So add something into your portfolio that will make sure such people receive some type of recognition after sharing their knowledge with others. But not everyone will be positively influenced by such recognition. Some people might prefer a more quiet acknowledgment over 15 seconds of fame.

Some people are motivated by guidelines. A job description that says that they should be sharing their knowledge might actually influence their behavior. In my experience, this is a small group. I would definitely not rely on this one working on a wider scale.

One of the first ideas I always hear mentioned is to give monetary rewards to "motivate" people. I have even heard statements like "Money is the only thing that will get people to contribute."

This is not true. In one example where people were given monetary rewards for sharing success stories, the result was a brief, temporary flow of contributions. A lot were in a form that did not provide much value without extensive rework. Clearly people often were focused on the incentive and not on the contribution.

One other problem is that people get the message that they need to be paid for sharing their knowledge. So as soon as the incentive goes down or is taken away, the sharing behavior will be worse than before. For an ongoing good knowledge flow, you need that ongoing participation, and you get that only if people accept it as part of their normal job. Thus monetary rewards can have negative effects in the long run. You will get quantity but not quality (unless very closely monitored—a costly and sometimes demotivating exercise).

Just as with other drivers, the best approach is a portfolio approach (i.e., motivating different people with different incentives). To reach as many as possible and to extend chances that incentives work, a combination of embedded processes (i.e., linked to objectives), recognition, and asynchronous rewards have worked best. By *asynchronous* I mean rewards that happen on certain occasions in contrast to *synchronous* rewards (monetary, as in "I share then I get something"). A good example of the effect of asynchronous rewards are lotteries. Have you ever seen how people storm into the ticket agencies when there is an unusually high jackpot? Their chances of winning are not higher, and if they win (especially if it is in a category below the jackpot), they will have to split the prize many times, because everyone else entered the lottery. High jackpots seem to be especially motivating, though. Similarly, I have seen occasional more visible rewards to be more successful than small invisible regular ones.

Apart from looking at *motivating factors*, I would recommend looking at the *demotivators* and fight those as an additional strategy. Instead of trying to directly *motivate* people, this approach attempts to ensure that any potential barriers or demotivators are reduced to a minimum. Motivation is a big challenge for anyone running knowledge flow management initiatives. The solution lies more in trying to get the obstacles removed from the flow than trying to make people do things. You can encourage and find compelling reasons for people to participate. But often it is more about identifying the key barriers that keep people from sharing their knowledge and work on reducing those.

WHAT IF YOUR KNOWLEDGE TAKES A WALK?

As knowledge is connected to humans, it can also easily flow out of your organization when people leave. A range of activities have been tried to *capture* that knowledge, but most of them are insufficient. You cannot store knowledge in a database, even though that is often one of the hopes that people have. You can store a certain amount of information shared by someone who had the knowledge, but it will not have the same value as the knowledge itself. There are many dimensions to knowledge that will be lost with the person. Recording stories, videos, and more might be a way to pick up some of the additional dimensions. A lot of the knowledge can be in the network a person was part of. It needs the connections that the person had with a given community. That type of knowledge actually would not completely take a walk but just get lost to a large degree.

The best way to keep knowledge from leaving the organization is to embed it. If a person with a specific knowledge is involved regularly in internal communities and works closely with other community members, a certain amount of knowledge becomes common knowledge (shared by multiple members of the community). If in that case the team member leaves, a lot of the knowledge stays in the organization.[3] This would not help if a competitor hires a whole community or team away from you, but such *group walks* are not as frequent as individual leavers.

Embedding the knowledge, as a side effect, also makes it less easy to replicate. Knowledge represented not by one person, but by the collaboration of a community is much harder for a competitor to replicate, even if it would hire away one or two key individuals.

For completeness, it must be said that the case of an individual who leaves and takes a certain amount of knowledge along does not necessarily have to be a bad thing. The case of someone leaving might enable *unlearning*, whereby people question existing knowledge and open up chances for seeing things in a new light. The remaining community could start to innovate after some old-way-thinking moved on. Also, if a certain expert is too dominant and people are too dependent on that person, it could hinder emancipation of others. Last but not least, the person who leaves might be replaced by someone external who introduces new thinking and innovation potential into the organization.

In this chapter I looked at some of the driving forces and strategies you could apply to actively drive improvements for your knowledge flow. The next chapter looks at the reverse side: barriers and how to get improvements by reducing them.

NOTES

1. The full quote reads: "What information consumes is rather obvious: it consumes the attention of its recipients. Hence a wealth of information creates a poverty of attention, and a need to allocate that attention efficiently among the overabundance of information sources that might consume it." Martin Greenberger, ed., *Computers, Communications and the Public Interest* (Baltimore, MD: The Johns Hopkins Press, 1971), pp. 40–41.

2. Tom H. Davenport and John C. Beck, *The Attention Economy: Understanding the New Currency of Business* (Boston: Harvard Business Press, 2002).

3. In project management, some people have been talking about a project *bus number*. This is the number of people who can get hit by a bus before the project is endangered. Others have transferred that concept to organizations; see: http://blog.tortus.com/2009/6/3/what-is-your-bus-number

CHAPTER **6**

Barriers

If a thing is worth doing, it is worth doing badly.
—G. K. Chesterton 1910, British Author and Journalist

To start the chapter, I want to explain why I chose the starting quote. The sentence that you probably have heard a lot more frequently is "If something is worth doing, it is worth doing right." Behind that quote stands a certain amount of perfectionism that is very often necessary to achieve extraordinary results.

But sometimes there is not enough time or resources to do it perfectly or even right. So the question is whether it is worth doing at all. It could be that with an 80 percent solution, you could be much better off than with a perfect solution that will never come. Speed is very important. Time to market is an important factor, whether externally to your customers or internally in competition with others in your organization.

It is worthwhile to realize that there are many situations where a suboptimal solution is actually more successful. I am not advocating striving for general mediocrity but for you to realize that a solution that misses its time to market might be useless, while one that hits the market quickly can create high value. One thing often overlooked is that results today are much more team oriented and collaborative then they were in the past. If you have a single actor creating something to be used in its final stage and have an organization that expects everything it receives in that final state, you will need people to produce near-perfect results. If instead you are building on collaborative forces (e.g., when building on social media and Web 2.0 technologies and processes), then handing something "imperfect" to the community "fast" can be a lot more valuable than if you held a contribution back just to improve on it in your hidden little office. One of the core principles of these types of knowledge exchanges is to have a high flow of knowledge, so you are better off with a larger number of building blocks versus a few black boxes.

The next sections discuss some aspects of this line of thinking including a look at quality and time-to-market delivery.

BARRIERS HINDERING THE FLOW

In a study on knowledge management by the Fraunhofer Institute,[1] one of the questions asked participants what barriers of knowledge management they see.

The top 10 responses were:

1. Lack of time
2. Missing knowledge management awareness
3. Missing awareness of knowledge
4. "Knowledge is power"
5. Missing reward systems
6. Missing transparency
7. Specialization
8. Inappropriate information technology (IT) structure
9. No organized knowledge sharing
10. Inappropriate company culture

The interesting part about the order of the responses was that the top two each got over 70 percent of the responses, while items 3 through 10 got only between 30 and 40 percent. So the two top barriers were seen as the major barriers for knowledge management to succeed.

I will discuss the top three in more detail and suggest some methods to attack those barriers.

1. **Lack of time.** Although the first item is formulated as "lack of time," I believe in reality it is "lack of priority." As we definitely do not have time for all activities that might be important, where we put our priorities becomes significant. If you want to really improve your knowledge flow, especially on the side where the knowledge enters the flow, and you are serious about it, you will need to make it a priority and ensure that employees have time to contribute. You can embed contribution into processes (e.g., as steps of a methodology). Another way to raise the priority is through clear goals that emphasize the value of leveraging knowledge. Leading by example drives some people to make things a priority because they might want to emulate management behavior.

2. **Missing knowledge management awareness.** This barrier speaks to the fact that people in your organization are not aware that sharing knowledge is even part of their job. They think it is something extra that they do on a Friday night, when their day job is done. It is not necessary that all knowledge flow management–related activities are visible under that label; in fact, it is actually a very good sign when they are so much embedded into standard processes that they are not visible anymore. But in the launch phases of any initiative, it is important that participants understand and are aware that there is an activity that they are specifically asked to engage in. They also need to understand that they will increase the value of the organization through participation. Methods to break down this barrier are marketing or embedding activities related to knowledge sharing into job descriptions, bonus plans, or review cycles.[2] Another way to raise the awareness is through stories that link business success to knowledge-sharing behavior or activity.

3. **Missing awareness of knowledge.** In the initiatives that I have run over the years, the effects of this barrier are most

interesting, and I think it is one that is often underestimated. What I have seen again and again is that people are not aware of their knowledge and specifically not aware of the real or potential value of their knowledge. In the ToolPool initiative, we have repeatedly experienced cases where somebody sends in a technical tool with a comment that goes as follows: "I am not sure if it worth anything to anybody, but if you think it is, why don't you publish it in ToolPool." And after we published it, it was downloaded hundreds of times by consultants worldwide. The first reason people underestimate the value of their contribution is that they overestimate its uniqueness. People tend to think that the challenge, and the need to look for a solution to it, happens only to them. More often than not, this is not the case. And even if there is a uniqueness to it, there are usually also commonalities, and users of that contribution can do some translation. They can pick up pieces of it, for example, and apply parts of it to their specific problem. There are a couple of methods to deal with this barrier:

- Create transparency. If people know in what ways and how frequently their contributions are reused, they tend to be surprised and the barrier slowly becomes smaller. Analysis and feeding that analysis back to the author is a great way to tackle this barrier.
- Having good knowledge intermediaries is another way to fight this barrier. Just by their experience, they can help to estimate the value of a contribution and motivate people to "risk" a contribution for the sake of potential benefit.

It was interesting to see that in 1997, the respondents to the survey considered the IT structure as significantly less important than a number of softer factors. Nevertheless, in the years after that survey, technology was very often the main point of focus.

I will not go into detail on all the barriers that made the list, but one that is worth a deeper discussion is the fourth, *knowledge is power*.

KNOWLEDGE IS POWER: HOW LONG?

This barrier is often mentioned because it inhibits people from sharing their knowledge. Their knowledge represents their value and seems to give them power; they believe that it will save them from becoming obsolete and getting fired. As a consequence, they have a tendency to hoard their knowledge. If this line of thinking is common with participants/employees, they are quite often on the wrong track.

Today's organization is much less about the knowledge you have. It is a lot more about the potential of knowledge that you can build. In the thirteenth century, the city of Venice moved all of its glassmaking facilities to the island of Murano in order to preserve the secret knowledge of glassmaking. It took until the end of the sixteenth century for the knowledge finally to slip out. At that time, Venice lost some of its power to its competition. In spite of harsh measures (i.e., death penalty for any glassmaking expert trying to leave), some of the knowledge made it into other parts of Europe, but there is still a lot of special expertise on Murano.

Things have changed since the thirteenth century. Most of the knowledge that people need today renews itself at breathtaking speed. Today we are talking more about days, months, maybe a few years but not centuries before knowledge might become obsolete. Due to this speed of change, it is usually dangerous for an individual to think that having knowledge represents power and to rely on it. The real power comes to those who are best at building and transferring knowledge, not at having knowledge. We are living in dynamic times. The most valuable people in the organization of the future are not those with knowledge that might be out-of-date tomorrow but those who are most capable of building new valuable knowledge. And to build knowledge, you need a network. But the network will not continue to share with you if you do not give something back. Hence it is those who invest in their network who are most likely to be good at building new (very much needed) knowledge. But people are often still stuck in the old model.

There is one more aspect to the "knowledge is power" barrier. I usually urge people to turn themselves into moving targets. One big misconception is that if I share my knowledge, the person I shared it with will automatically be at the same level as I. But as I explained before, this is not true; there is no one-to-one knowledge transfer. So I share some information with somebody, who then needs to re-create knowledge in his head out of that information. People learn during the sharing process. Learning happens during the formulation of the information about the knowledge I want to share. I usually learn something every time I formulate the information, and by doing so, I am basically getting ahead of where I was the minute I started the sharing process.

Those who are very much afraid of competition often underestimate this effect. They fear that the person they share with will use the information to get ahead. But through the complete learning that comes from frequent interactions, you can turn yourself into a moving target. Each individual you share with gain from the information, but you can get even further ahead in your area of expertise. Some recent studies confirm what I have experienced over the years.[3]

These effects are often not visible. Via some education, stories, and examples, you can educate people to realize how wrong they are. In some cases, it is also a matter of getting the right people into your organization. It could very well be the smarter choice to pick people who show potential to build knowledge in dynamic environments over those with knowledge from the past.

SHARING KNOWLEDGE TAKES EFFORT

For a good flow of knowledge, there needs to be sufficient input. But sharing information in a way that others can create new knowledge from it does not come for free.[4] It will always need effort. Expecting that this process will happen without additional effort would be like asking for a perpetual motion machine, producing energy output without any energy input. Nevertheless I have found that often stakeholders expect that sharing knowledge is possible without spending any extra effort. As a result there is no plan or budget for the effort but a clear expectation that there will be positive outcomes.

Those expectations are unrealistic. It is important to acknowledge that there are barriers to overcome. It takes time and effort to talk to somebody, to lay down information in documents or produce assets that then can be moved around the organization and used as pointers to experts. If you acknowledge that a certain amount of effort needs to be spent, you can start looking at ways to minimize that effort.

Sometimes people want to share, but they want to expend almost zero effort doing so. But if people do not put any effort into the sharing, the contribution is often of very limited value. In the ToolPool initiative, for example, people might complain about the time it takes to describe a tool in a good introduction. However, everyone expects that the tools *they* explore will all start with a great introduction. A good introduction and categorization are very hard to produce automatically. Sometimes people complain about missing information in others' contributions, but their own contributions lacked the necessary diligence as well.

More effort is not always better. The trick is to shoot for the perfect amount of effort to get the best possible output for that effort. Finding the best effort-to-result ratio needs regular tuning of processes. Finding that right balance is critical as spending effort of this type represents cost to the organization. You want to minimize the cost but maximize the result. If you tune effort to zero, you will not get any value; if the effort is too high, you might get great contributions, but at what cost? Is it worth it for those involved in day-to-day activities to spend that much time on sharing their knowledge and cut into other activities? At the same time, conditions change constantly. People get more sophisticated, topics change, or you are facing different and changing cultures. This is why continuously looking at the effort–output equation is very important. Analyze frequently whether you are asking too much from your contributors and might lose them, or if you are not asking enough of them and might lose the ones who are expecting a certain level of output quality.

A quick word on quality. This is an area where people often say: "In my knowledge initiative, I only want the highest-quality knowledge being shared." I do not want to dispute that quality is important. In an ideal world, all contributions are very nicely prepared and present extremely useful knowledge. But you have to define what quality you are talking about. With ToolPool, we primarily have two types of qualities: technical and contribution quality.

1. Technical Quality
   - Is it immediately ready to use?
   - What is the effort/time saved by using that tool?
   - Is it well rounded and 100 percent in line with the current company strategy?
   - Does it contain an extensive and complete set of technical documentation?

   The issue with this type of quality is that it might sometimes be hard or at least very costly to judge or predict. If you focus too hard on this type of quality, you might cut out some innovative ideas, just because they are not perfectly prepared. If you can get that quality, I am all for it, but if you cannot, it should not be a reason to pass up contributions.

2. Contribution Quality
   - Does it have a concise but sensible introduction and some describing parameters to be able to find it?
   - Does it follow a minimum documentation standard such that those considering reuse can easily and quickly decide if this is worth a second look?
   - Does the minimum documentation feature information about limitations as well?
   - Does it provide some visuals that make it easy for people to imagine if they might want to reuse it?
   - Are contact details complete, so those interested can reach out for further information and clarification?
   - Are all authors properly acknowledged?

   Contribution quality is a lot easier/cheaper to judge than technical quality. I am not saying that technical quality should not be considered. If a contribution is clearly technically poor (and we check that by having experts look over contributions), it should not pass the contribution process. But very often it is hard to predict the real potential value of a contribution. For innovation purposes, I would be careful not to be too strict about it. It has been amazing how often something that looked very simple and standard inspired people to do innovative things or extract pieces from the full contribution that turned out to be excellent reusable components.

With contribution quality, however, you should be rather strict. Otherwise, you are endangering the potential that somebody can pick it up, judge it, and finally reuse it. With a poor contribution quality, you are limiting the chance that someone will put in the effort to learn more about the contribution.

To tune the effort-to-outcome ratio, it is important to check where the effort is spent and whether it is actually a smart effort. If people are asked to spend a lot of effort to prepare a contribution or provide support information with it and it is never used, the effort would have been wasted.

It is not easy to get the tuning right, but I always try to teach contributors to think about their contribution not like a *contributor* but as if they were a *reuser*. Contributors should keep in mind the basic and most important pieces of information *they* would expect from someone's contribution. It is fine to make it easy for yourself, but put some smart effort into making it easy for users. Put yourself into their shoes.

A very good example to illustrate this point comes from a few years back with ToolPool. A consultant sent in a tool (a collection of SAS programs) and she had put in some effort to write a special service routine to package the tool. While from her point of view, this type of *packaging* service routine was very useful, it would have been more sensible to provide a service routine that *unpackaged* the tool. She was probably one of very few who needed to change the tool and then repackage it; likely there were hundreds who needed to reuse the tool; all they needed was to unpackage it.

Often it is not about more or less effort but the *right* effort. Knowledge intermediaries can help to tune the effort on a case-by-case basis by working with contributors to help them find a good balance of effort to outcome.

I NEED TWO MORE WEEKS

Very often when I ask a consultant to give me one of his cool tools, the response is "Sure, I am happy to share it, but I need two more weeks." Fact is, these people very rarely ever find time (it does not become a priority) to finish the tool. You may get it within a year or perhaps never. A year from now the knowledge represented by the tool might be outdated, and it might have missed the time to market completely. The turnover of knowledge and information is increasing. So if getting a tool takes too long, it might be useless by the time other employees receive it, or many others may have reinvented the wheel, wasting time, money, and opportunity.

Instead of giving the potential contributors two weeks, I encourage them to contribute the tool *now*; in the documentation under limitations/notes, they should write down what they would be doing if they had two more weeks.

If they contribute the tool and someone else uses it, that user knows that it is *not* perfect, since the status has been indicated. For example, say Consultant A provides a tool that is missing features a, b, and c. The author puts the tool out there, describing in a positive way its limitations. Consultant B finds the tool and thinks, "Well, not bad, but I need features a and b." So she uses the tool as a basis and develops features a and b on top of what she picked up. Here comes the big difference to Consultant A adding features a and b. Consultant A would have done it on normal company time or maybe in free time on the weekend. If Consultant B needs the features of the tool for a customer, likely she will develop it as part of a project; that is usually paid time. This is a much more effective method. Because it is in a real project, it is a lot more likely that features a and b are implemented not how a consultant *thinks* it should be done but how a customer really needs it. And if things work out well, Consultant B will contribute the enhanced tool back to ToolPool, or at a minimum let Consultant A know that she actually did features a and b. Together they might figure out how to best contribute it so others who might find it useful can also get it.

Because a tool might get shared early, a lot of people might think that the quality of the contribution might be poor. However, this brings up a good question on how to define quality. Knowledge quality is very hard, if not impossible, to judge because a small raw idea can be much more valuable than a cleaned-up and finished big programming system that is seldom needed or hard to fit into existing environments. This type of quality is dependent on the person judging it. It is difficult to predict if something will be a success or not. Spending a lot of effort to get it to a level that I call "presumed perfect" could be a waste of time

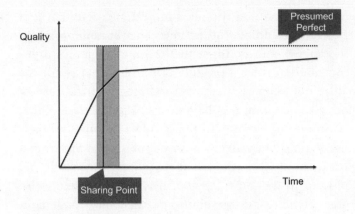

Exhibit 6.1 The Sharing Point

and effort. I am not trying to encourage the production of low-quality material, but without an easy way to judge a tool's worth, trying to focus on finished contributions only can be too limiting.

Exhibit 6.1 exemplifies what often happens during the creation of a potential contribution. A consultant has a great idea and implements it rather quickly, getting a good amount of functionality done in only a few days. The functionality/quality curve rises sharply. At one point the curve flattens; it takes more and more effort to standardize and raise a tool to perfection, which it never reaches. For innovation, a good time to share is in the time frame depicted by the shaded area. There is no perfect sharing point, but picking one in that area has some advantages.

When we looked at more detail on how people reuse contributions in ToolPool, we found that unless it is a small component or a complete system, they will not be able to reuse it exactly as is. With some exceptions, they will need to adapt it to the specific (and dynamically changing) environment of the customer they are working for. So if Consultant A puts really big efforts into ensuring that the tool is "standardized" and cleans it up to be really nice looking before contributing, there is a likelihood that Consultant B, who picks it up, will spend a considerable time to restandardize it for his customer potentially pulling out changes that were added based on preferences that Consultant A had. In that case the effort is wasted twice.

There are reasons other than the need-more-time argument that keep people from contributing. Sometimes the argument might be—and this is somewhat in contrast to the time-to-market argument—that a contribution is for a product or solution that is not the very latest or does not support the current strategy. In the case of solutions to older products, you will have to ask: How likely is it that there will be a customer problem with that product? From a marketing point of view, you do not want to push old messages, but from a technical support point of view you are likely to have customers still using a solution prior to the latest version. It is not possible or wise to force an upgrade in all cases; sometimes it can be very convenient to have a solution for this older product that the customer dearly loves or is not ready to throw out.

Similarly, when you have a solution that does not support the current strategy, you could either police it or position it:

- **Police it.** Do not let it into your knowledge base.
- **Position it.** Let it in but with proper positioning on how and when it should or should not be used.

I have found the positioning approach to be the smarter one. Realistically it is hard to control knowledge that appears very valuable to some people by trying to ignore its existence. If you cut it out of the open knowledge-sharing process, it will usually trade under the table. In contrast, if you let it enter your initiative but add a clear positioning, you are bringing it into the open. People will know it is there, but they will also know that they should be making use of the contribution in only very limited situations, if at all. Positioning should always include a pointer to the official supported version that is fully in line with strategy. The knowledge will flow whenever people see value in it, no matter if they are correct or if it supports current strategy. You can divert that flow into the main knowledge stream that you are managing, or you can let it sink under the surface.

LESS CAN BE MORE

When creating a flow of knowledge via an initiative, how much of the existing knowledge do you want in that stream? The obvious answer seems to be "as much as possible." This is not always the case, however. If your strategy is to go for quantity, you often sacrifice quality. If you are driving for as much as possible, you will usually use motivational elements (such as incentives) that will get some people to contribute things for the sake of contributing and not for the sake of potential value. I usually call that "throwing a contribution over the fence." With growing quantity, you often get an even faster-growing need for quality control. And quality control of bad-quality contributions can be rather frustrating in comparison to processing high quality contributions. You are usually better off relying on a self-driven contribution instead of beating people to come up with some stuff to make their numbers or get that incentive you put out.

There is another issue with high numbers: attention. As part of ToolPool, we send a weekly e-mail to about 1,600 technical people worldwide every Sunday. Announcing between 5 and 15 new and updated ToolPool contributions per week produces a manageable e-mail that people like and find time to browse through. If the same e-mail had 100 new entries, you might think that it would be of higher value. But most people would not even read the first 5 to 15, as they are overwhelmed with the choices offered. The best you might get is that they scan over it but do not have time to look at any of them in more detail. From an attention point of view, I strongly believe that less can be more.

There is a similar effect on the contribution side of things. When you are asking for contributions and want 100 parameters (meta-information), a lot of people might give up at the third parameter, because they are overwhelmed and frustrated by what is ahead of them. If, however, you are asking for 10 parameters, you are more likely to get 9 good ones, and 9 are better than 3.

Usually the quality of the meta-information for each of the parameters is also better with a small manageable set. Finding the right amount needs regular tuning. This is not always easy to do if there are systems involved. Systems are not always flexible enough to add/remove or change the meta-information structure.

Therefore, it is best to err on the low side and be firm on pushing back on requirements from somebody who is asking for all those parameters, especially if it is not clear whether the information will ever be used. Also, define parameters in an open way to cope with future changes. You are putting so much effort into launching and embedding an initiative that you want it to survive long term. This is possible, however, only if you are not getting tied down in today's details and are open for the future.

The less-is-more theme can also be applied to system interfaces and underlying processes. Start with a smaller set of features, but make the interface flexible so users have room for adapting to changing processes, possibly by customizing the interface itself. Processes should be flexible as well to cope with changing conditions.

Collect frequent feedback and enhance the interface in small steps based on user input. The average user will be happier with the simple interface than with something overloaded that does not provide any immediate value. Of course, less is not the only guiding rule. Often users want the "perfect" amount of information in front of them. Not more and not less. Unfortunately, that perfect amount is different for different people, and what is considered good presentation will vary as well.

Portals are an example because they can be a flexible system that allows for customization. But a note of caution regarding customization: An argument often heard from the technical side is "This system is perfect because the users can customize it anyway they want." In reality, the majority of users (who often are a lot less technical than the designers) do not want to customize, they want it to magically have the perfect interface without having to spend a lot of time on anything not related to the actual business process. That presents a certain dilemma regarding the customization scheme. So customization would need to be extremely simple.[5] Alternatively, one idea would be to employ a knowledge intermediary in a role I call the portal customization coach. This person would be an expert on customization and would go sit with every new (or role-changing) employee and assist in product customization. Just as we have ergonomics consultants help us set up desk, chair, and equipment to be optimal from an efficiency and health point of view, portal customization coaches would set up the information ergonomics. This is a great example of a role that the human resources function should look into creating.

LEGAL LIMITATIONS

To have knowledge flowing, information needs to be exchanged. And usually the idea is to increase the flow, but one barrier is increasingly becoming an issue in many organizations, especially those bound to strict rules of what can be exchanged (i.e., government organizations, pharmaceutical companies, or financial institutions). Laws or regulations will be the reason for having to limit the knowledge flow.

One area where these limits are becoming more evident is in global companies, where the interaction from country to country is growing but information exchange is kept within boundaries, either geographic or divisional.

I am by no means a legal expert, so I will not go into great detail on the issues. In general, I would emphasize that those driving knowledge flow management need to be in regular contact with their legal department and involve them in strategy building. Integrating legal processes can cut into some of the desired freedom, but the consequences for the whole knowledge flow management program could be disastrous if legal limits are ignored. Some examples of where those limits might apply are:

- Customer information cannot be shared across countries.

- Employee information is often protected under country laws. This can vary from country to country, and you might have to go by the lowest denominator in a global initiative, which can be frustrating for those used to more liberal laws.

- Import/export restrictions can apply for information just as much as for products (e.g., descriptions of encryption algorithms that are not allowed to be shared from the United States to certain countries).

- Intellectual property rights or nondisclosure agreements with customers or partners can limit information sharing.

Those are just some examples. The details of what is allowed and what is not can be complicated, and can also change over time, based on new regulations, laws, or bilateral agreements between countries.

But there are some general ideas on how you can tackle this barrier to at least some degree:

■ As mentioned earlier, there is a difference between information and knowledge. The information itself might be protected, but there is still a possibility that at a higher and more general level, the knowledge and the experience that has been obtained during a given process can be raised to a more abstract level. Information related to that higher-level knowledge might still be sharable. For example, you might not be allowed to share detailed information about a customer project, but some of the general discoveries you made during the project could well be safe to share.

■ Create legal awareness with those driving the initiatives but also with those involved in the contribution and usage processes on a daily basis. For ToolPool, for example, we integrated a process that automatically sends every contribution meeting certain criteria that mandate legal checking to a special contact in the legal department. This happens as the first step before further processing begins. It does slow down the overall process, but the overhead is definitely worth the reduced risk.

■ Find a good balance between central control and local responsibility. Central control is helpful, but the individuals involved in a knowledge-sharing process have to be aware that they have personal responsibility as well. There is no way to get full control of employees' actions. As a result, it is important to communicate the responsibilities and train participants on legal issues, such as export laws and intellectual property rights.

As we have seen, there are a number of barriers that can inhibit organizational knowledge flow. Reducing those barriers is one way to improve your flow. Motivated by some of the drivers, people often like to share their knowledge. The barriers could be holding them back. Therefore, managing the barriers is a good way to positively influence the flow.

NOTES

1. Hans-Jörg Bullinger, Kai Woerner, and Juan Prieto, "Wissensmanagement Heute," Fraunhofer Institut für Arbeitswirtschaft und Organisation, Stuttgart, Germany, 1997.
2. Note that this type of addition to performance-related documents and processes does not usually drive the behavior directly, as many incorrectly believe, but you can

raise awareness in this way. A more detailed discussion follows in Chapter 8 about measuring.

3. "Fact is that those that ongoing share their knowledge have a better network, get better support from their colleagues, and usually outperform those that are less integrated and do hoard their knowledge. In economic downturns IBM recommends to have people increase their social network and better capture their knowledge" (www-935.ibm.com/services/us/gbs/bus/pdf/gbe03120-usen-hcm-economic.pdf).

4. The term *knowledge sharing* is meant to represent the process by which information is exchanged and based on that information new knowledge is created by the receiver of that information. In the end portions of the knowledge are *shared* between sender and receiver.

5. A good example is the way gadgets (those little windows that you use to present news streams and other RSS feeds) can be placed and manipulated on iGoogle.

CHAPTER **7**

The Technology Trap

The knowledge of the world is only to be acquired in the world, and not in a closet.

—Lord Chesterfield (1694–1773), published 1774

Based on the flawed use of the term *knowledge management* to depict the management of an entity external to humans, a number of organizations approached the original issue of making best use of the knowledge within their organization from an information technology (IT) perspective. Many knowledge management projects have been started within the IT organization, and not too surprisingly they began with the evaluation and buying of software and hardware. This was true 10 years ago, but in a lot of cases it is still true today. Again and again, one of the first questions I get when I talk to those who have been charged with creating or reviving a knowledge management program and who are just getting started is "What software did you use?" When I investigate further, it is very clear that people think that all they have to do is buy and install the right software to be successful. The software question should be one of the last ones I am asked, not the first one.

But if we look back, the situation looked like this (do not feel bad if this is how your company approached it; you are definitely not alone):

111

A middle manager (Joe) encounters the potential value of knowledge management (via a conference, article, or book).

Joe goes back to his company, discusses it with others, and gets some excitement and buy-in from his boss. He then initiates a new project, appointing a project manager (Bill).

Bill and a few others do some additional research and stumble over a few knowledge management vendors.

Before they have planned a fully holistic view of what this might mean to their company culture and how they are going to deal with the ongoing issues, they invite three or four vendors to showcase their knowledge management software.

Companies A, B, C come in to show their super-polished portals, content management, or collaboration platforms, carefully demonstrating how great the systems look if they are filled with information that can be retrieved at a click of a button. At the same time they are just as carefully steering around any questions on issues you might have to fill the back end of that portal with useful, up-to-date, clean information on a daily basis via processes integrated into the normal day-job of your employees.

Everybody evaluating the software is very excited; the return on investment of saving time and avoiding reinventing the wheel and the innovation potential of such a system filled by thousands of employees dwarfs the $1.5 million that it will cost you. Well, your budget was only $1 million, but that extension is easy to argue.

The system gets installed, and IT support is handled by a few technically savvy geeks who just love to explore the 324 features the new software has to offer.

The roll-out is done in a strategic way. Everything is tested to make sure that technically it is working perfectly at the big launch. After all, this is an important and strategic project. A high-level vice president or even the president either sends out a special message or introduces it at some kickoff presentation. The internal communications group produces and runs a news article about the way that the new knowledge management system will make everybody more efficient and how it will now be so easy to find all the *knowledge* they need. It will be only a few clicks away.

Usually the expectancy will be that everyone will immediately go to the new system and start sharing their knowledge.

And some people will do that. Some will share the excitement and start entering information representing some of their knowledge.

Just as typical is the situation 18 months down the road. The system is still there. It contains some content, usually entered once, seldom updated. There are a few users—usually a fraction of the number of people anticipated. The original team that developed and rolled it out has left the company or is on other projects within the organization. If you ask people about it, they will say things like "Oh yes, I remember we had something like that, but I am not sure if it is still there and where it is."

So what went wrong? They forgot the engine in the car!

If we take a car as an analogy for a moment, what happened is a little bit like buying a car that has a lot of luxury items. It has alloy wheels and all the internal extras (power-everything, 500-watt stereo, leather seats); however, you buy it without an engine. As a result, it will just sit there. The car without the engine was already $45,000, so there was no money left for the engine. It would have cost another $5,000.

But as we all know a car without an engine misses the point. What I am claiming is that a knowledge-sharing or knowledge flow initiative without investing in a lasting team to run the show not only from a technical support perspective, but with the right strategy, ongoing support, frequent application adaption, internal marketing, and motivational activities, is like buying a car without an engine. If getting knowledge to flow was your objective, without those elements, you did not give yourself much of a chance.

For every dollar you spend on the technology, you need to spend at least 50 cents for the ongoing initiative support. And that is considering that you got well-experienced professionals running your knowledge flow management initiative.

This can be illustrated by the following, Leistner's first law of knowledge flow management:

$$K = T + S$$

where

> K = Full investment for a knowledge flow management initiative
>
> T = Technology investment
>
> S = Initiative support investment

For a successful initiative, I am proposing the following relationship, where the investment into initiative support should be at least half the amount that is spent for technology. Ideally the amount spent should be close to the same amount that you spend on technology.

$$0.5 \times T < S < T$$

This relationship can vary depending on the type of initiative. It will also vary over the time that an initiative is running. Once basic technology is in place, S should grow a bit higher than T. This formula is most important in the launch year.

It is essential to realize that S is not just technical support. While some of that is necessary, the technical portion should only be small portion. Most of it should be spent on the process and drivership support.

As mentioned earlier, technology is often easier to introduce and embed than processes. As soon as the focus shifts to human behavior, the situation becomes more complex. Or at least for those who lack a proper understanding of how to deal with human behavior, it seems a lot more complex. In some cases, the actual knowledge exchange can be simpler in a face-to-face situation, but there is no obvious handle for control in such processes, which makes it complex.

Because many knowledge management projects were driven primarily by technically focused people, it is easy to see why the focus was on the technical side. The human side of why people might participate or not and what could be done to get their ongoing involvement is something that needs a specific skills set and experience, as discussed earlier.

Do not misunderstand me: I believe technology is very important. It is a great enabler, and its existence can actually change people's behavior over time, as we have seen with some of the Web 2.0 technologies. The question is to what degree is that achieved by technology alone. Just building something and putting it in front of people is not enough. No matter how easy it is, it needs some type of guidance to be really efficient. Without that guidance, you might get good usage but potentially not very efficient usage. What good is it if you have large participation, because people find your technology easy to use, but they are not using it in a way that creates business value? You might think in that case that the *system* is insufficient, as it does not guide the user enough through a business process. As discussed, locking the business process too heavily into the system would create another big long-term problem because it would not allow enough flexibility.

ASSET OR POINTER?

But how should you guide people to use the flexibility? What are typical mistakes, and what guidance should you give? One good example would be the customization support for portals mentioned in Chapter 6, representing a more general support on how to use technology efficiently.

One other category of guidance is around the role that technology actually plays. The next story illustrates how viewing a system in one way or another can make a big difference.

In one of the earlier years of ToolPool, a consultant asked on a mailing list for a tool that would produce automatic process documentation as an add-on to one of our products. In the request she sent out, she mentioned that she had found a version of the tool that worked with a prior release of the software, but she needed it for the very latest release. It was Friday morning and she needed it rather urgently; without having such a tool, the project might be delayed.

When I saw her e-mail, I privately (directly) replied to her, asking whether she had contacted the author to ask if an update already existed. She had not done so. When she asked the author, it turned out that he already had the updated version but had not found time to contribute it yet, but he could send it to her. Within hours she had exactly what she needed, her project stayed on track, and the ToolPool team, aware of the update, supported the author to get it into ToolPool for everybody as soon as possible.

Many people looking at a "knowledge base" think of it as a repository of knowledge. If they cannot find what they are looking for or if it is really not there, the reaction is to turn away and in the worst case they start reinventing the wheel. But any such system is actually more than just a repository; it is what I refer to as a *repository of pointers to the one who knows.*

In the example, the consultant was looking for a certain knowledge asset that was not in the repository, but the older entry was a great pointer to the person who had the solution. In other cases, the solution might not be a new version of a tool; it could be that the author of the contribution has some specific knowledge that could be of value.

The contribution itself is only an incomplete representation of the knowledge that a contributor has, but it serves well as a pointer. In fact, often people acknowledge that they actually prefer to talk to an expert than look at some document or pick up something contributed into a database. Often people prefer to go directly to the person who has the knowledge. In a large global organization, this method does not scale well; it can be very tough to find that person. One approach might be to use some type of skills database or enhanced staff directory system that records skill and experience levels. Often such systems have a data quality problem. Participants are supposed to fill in their profiles but do not do it regularly and consistently enough. But even if you get over that problem by using enough drivers to ensure sufficient quality (as we managed with the skills database at SAS), you have to be clear that such systems map only one out of an endless number of dimensions of a person's knowledge. As long as you understand those limitations, a skills database can serve a number of purposes.

However, a collection of an author's contributions represents a work product that covers additional dimensions. For example, when a consultant indicated in the skills database that she knows product X at level 3, which is defined in detail as being able to perform certain tasks with the product, it might be somewhat one-dimensional. If the same consultant indicated via a different skills database item that she also knows a certain computer operating system, you would have additional information useful in a search for a given expert.

Now if the same person has made several contributions around the product, those contributions represent a pointer to certain knowledge that the consultant would have to have in order to produce what she contributed. Her contributions represent a few more dimensions of her knowledge that make it easier to identify her.

Often users do not look at knowledge repositories in this way. They see the repository and that is where it stops. If they do not find the right asset to use, they assume nothing is available. Their thinking has to go further, and they need to look beyond the repository that is in front of them. This limited view can be considered the *asset view*; the one that views contributions as pointers can be thought of as the *pointer view*.

Recently, through the use of Web 2.0 type of tools, people seem to be getting more used to this type of connecting to experts via pointers. In fact, Twitter, the immensely growing microblogging service, is based largely on people taking a pointer view. Each individual Twitter message with its 140 characters is too small to represent full answers, but it can also be a pointer to a person with more expertise.

One of the Twitter accounts that I follow is from somebody offering tips for competitive swimmers. The first pointer to that person was a small tweet (Twitter message) that a friend pointed out to me. That tweet led me to the actual person twittering, and I decided it would be worthwhile to follow that person. In this case it was actually a combination of pointers: A human (my friend) pointed me to a system, which in turn contained a pointer to another human.

The pointer view is important, and I recommend that all participants of a knowledge flow management initiative should understand it. It ties back to the quality argument. Say there are contributions that are not complete and leave open questions; therefore, they are not considered of value by those who only look at it from using the repository view. Under the pointer view, though, that same contribution could actually be a key pointer to an expert, and the fact that there is an open question could well inspire direct contact. Once the direct contact is established (via e-mail, telephone, or in person), more of the tacit knowledge could flow, some of which is between the lines. A document itself could not have provided that type of transfer. In an extreme case, an imperfect contribution could raise the chances that two humans connect with each other, but that is taking it a little far. (Note that I am not advocating producing low quality to inspire direct contact.)

TOOLS: NOT ONLY TECHNOLOGY

For the remainder of this chapter, the word *tools* is used in a slightly different fashion than in previous chapters. So far it has been used to depict contributions within the ToolPool case study. But just as you have tools in a software environment, you can speak of tools to be used to enhance organizational knowledge flow. As you will see, some of those "tools" are technology based and others are just methods that do not necessarily need any technology to support them.

The tools I discuss are only a selection and by no means a complete list of everything you could or should use. But these examples cover different aspects of a knowledge flow. Some of them will be familiar, others might be new, or you might not have thought of them in that way before. Some of the latest tools, such as blogs, wikis, and networking platforms, are not covered in this chapter but are discussed in the context of Web 2.0 and social media in Chapter 9.

Each tool is looked at from the point of view on how it can support the knowledge flow. To discuss any one of them in detail would take much more than a section in a chapter; however, there are a number of books dedicated to tools and concepts such as Communities of Practice and Storytelling, for example.[1]

CoPs

Communities of practice (CoPs) are one of the most important concepts when it comes to enhancing knowledge flow, especially when there is considerable tacit knowledge is involved in whatever the members of the community practice on a daily basis. CoPs are largely centered around humans and their interaction. Nevertheless, some people still manage to turn them into a primarily technological topic. Recently a colleague told me that he had this CoP for "topic X." When I asked some more questions, it turned out that basically all he had was a mailing list around "topic X" that he was managing.

A mailing list might be one of many tools that you could use to *support* your CoP, but it is definitely not a CoP in itself. In the days prior to the Web, some mailing lists were probably a good backbone that helped a community to exchange ideas. But the actual CoP is a group of people who are practicing common things or has some common understanding. The individuals within the CoP usually play one or multiple roles; the key is that membership is defined by that common interest or knowledge. Membership happens by invitation or self-selection but not by organizational structure or mandate. Etienne Wenger, who is one of the fathers of CoPs, often refers to them as the way that work really happens. They are an organizational structure that sometimes can be invisible but nevertheless plays an important role in letting knowledge flow around the organization.

As a CoP is not bound to organizational structures, it can span the boundaries and silos that exist in the organization due to bureaucracy or politics. Because members of the community focus more on the topical issues, they find a common ground in the CoP that enables them to develop the type of trust needed to share across boundaries.

CoPs could exist completely without technology support based only on face-to-face interaction between community members. But in today's global organizations, where scaling is one of the success factors, they are often spread around the globe. To permit the needed connectivity, a number of technologies, such as mailing lists, video or telephone conferences, and virtual meeting places, will play an enabler role.

Analogous to the need to drive a knowledge flow management initiative using support roles, a CoP needs drivership. It needs a passionate leader to get started and survive the bootstrap phase. But it also needs other supporting functions to survive long term.

SKILLS MANAGEMENT

In 1998 I was working at the European headquarter of SAS in Heidelberg, Germany. At the time we had a central organization that was doing product marketing but was also responsible for knowledge transfer from headquarters to the different countries across Europe. Knowledge transfer was done via central or local training and by sending headquarter experts into the offices to work side by side with local people. After some time it became clear that the headquarters function could not cover all the engagements and that it would be better to add local experts to the pool of those going out to support projects.

Two issues prompted us to look into some type of skills management system:

1. How should you plan the training? How many people are up to speed with the latest products and solutions?

2. Where would you find those local experts whom you might want to lend out to those offices that need them?

To answer those questions and get a central overview, we needed some way to collect skill levels from local consultants. So the idea of a skills database was born. The very first version of this skills database was very simple, and the technology support was rudimentary. We basically had consultants fill in spreadsheets with a list of skills and a simple rating category (Novice/Advanced/Expert/Guru); then local personnel would transfer that data into a simple Web application. The centrally stored data could then be used for searches, reporting, and analysis. The list of competencies was one-dimensional. The descriptions of the four levels were the same across all skills entered. We dealt with only a specific kind of staff: consultants. While the system was simple, we developed a number of processes that got more and more sophisticated with experience. The simple skills database worked well, but over time it turned out that there was definitely room for improvement.

The data entry performed by agents for the person who had the skill turned out to be cumbersome. The descriptions were too broad; we needed more ways of defining rating categories for different types of skills. There were some other areas where we identified ways to improve processes and the system itself.

An assessment with users (consultants, managers, and administrators) revealed that we actually would be best off by designing a new system, taking the gained experiences into account. That new system, the ESDB (employee skills database), was developed interactively with constant involvement of the user community. The programming started out using a method called extreme programming, where two developers worked side by side for months to come up with a modular and flexible design that we are still building on today to extend the system. But the ESDB did not evolve on technical ideas and comments as much as it did through the constant feedback from its users.

One of the key ideas was to build standard profiles of skills for each of the staff groups. As those relate to certain type of jobs, we call those *job families*. So each member of a job family gets the same set of skills to choose from. They evaluate themselves on a subset of the whole list—only those that apply—and their manager reviews and approves the profile before it can be searched. Based on people's concerns, several levels of confidentiality were introduced and special roles were created that have different views and capabilities within the ESDB.

In the early years I went through a few discussions with knowledge management experts from other organizations about skills management systems in general. If people had used them, they usually said they did not get as much out of them as they had expected, mostly due to data quality issues and participation problems.

As mentioned in Chapter 5, by using multiple drivers and integrating the system into multiple initiatives (skills management, resource sharing, and training development), we have been able to overcome those problems to a large extent. With the success of the initiatives, our skills database has turned out to be a success as well.

What made it successful was an adjusted expectancy of what skills management could deliver. If the expectation is that you will have every skill of those involved perfectly mapped at all times, you will easily get disappointed. If, however, you need a way to identify prime candidates for a short list to be qualified further using human judgment and interaction, you can be successful. It is another case of the human–technology continuum, where *not* shooting for 100 percent technology but striking a good balance between human activity and technology can be the key to success.

"KNOWLEDGE BASES"

In Chapter 1 we discussed the fact that there is actually no such thing as a *knowledge base*, because knowledge cannot be stored in a database. But it was also mentioned that it would be unrealistic to expect that this terminology will go away soon. One possible way to put the term back into the perspective of an organizational knowledge flow could be to envision a knowledge base as a database of information that could be used to create new knowledge and also serve as a repository of pointers to the one who knows.

If you understand that distinction and operate any initiatives involving such a knowledge base accordingly, a knowledge base actually might prove to be valuable. But this will be true only if the surrounding processes cover all the human and motivational aspects that enable the creation of new knowledge and if key stakeholders understand the nature of what they are working with.

Knowledge bases can be a supportive piece of a full initiative that enables scaling and global reach. Like any repository, they usually are only as good as the content that they contain. The value of that content could be in the contribution itself or the potential value of serving as a pointer to the one who knows. The emphasis needs to be on getting good information into the knowledge bases by motivating the right individuals to share key pointers to the knowledge they possess.

PORTALS

Intranet portals, sometimes referred to just as *portals*, are usually Web sites that bring together a range of sources into one Web page. As the name indicates, they are supposed to be the entrance to a wide range of information sources. But unlike a normal entrance, a portal actually represents not one but many doors, each door an opening to an information stream that could be kept internal or external to an organization but is brought together into one common interface. The portal itself would not store much of the information but only bring it together. One of the key functions of portals is that they usually are customizable. They offer a standard set of presented sources that can then be altered by an administrator or the users themselves. And the modifications usually happen at different levels. You can change the actual information streams that are presented. As an example, you might be able to select from a range of internal streams (company news, sales status numbers, events, cafeteria menus) as well as external streams (general and industry news, competitor watch lists, weather). The portal designer or portal administrator can also lock some streams to ensure that they are always present.[2] Customization means the users could:

- **Subset or customize the streams.** A good example of a customized stream might be a subset on a news stream. Instead of all the news flowing in via that stream, the user could choose a subset based on a given condition.

- **Change frequencies and refresh rates.** Instead of updating the stream whenever something new appears, the user could choose to get it updated only once a day.

- **Adapt the appearance.** This could mean that the user would be able to move the different stream presentations (*portlets*) around on the main pane (the *desktop*). It could also mean customizing titles, colors, sizes, and so on.

Portals are often mentioned as a component in knowledge management as they provide a way to link into multiple *knowledge management systems*. But remember: What is represented remains information; it is not knowledge. The portal might open a way to interact with others, which in the end could result in some type of knowledge exchange via information. Also, as portals offer a range of information, they can be seen as a good tool to bring together the right streams to produce new knowledge.

Portals have become a lot more flexible in recent years, through the wider distribution of RSS channels.[3]

With the use of RSS and smarter portlets, it has become very easy to present streams in the portlet without any programming.

One thing to understand very clearly about portals is that the value is under the hood. To come back to the analogy of the car without an engine, this is a similar case. A portal might be great looking, but it is only a presentation layer. It lives and dies with the underlying information: the streams and how they are filled. For that matter, you could show a great portal in a demonstration that is filled with some example information. People see those portlets and can imagine how they might look with their own information, offering all those valuable resources that might be out there around their organization. But they often underestimate the effort needed to get from the demonstration to a functional ongoing and valuable portal. I have seen many demonstrations that overlook the need for those efforts and focus solely on the output side of the application. But how does all that useful information get into the portal? Who drives the strategy on what type of information streams should be feeding the portal and how should they be integrated and presented. Who is in charge of maintaining the streams themselves and their sensible integration? Who manages common dimensions in a way that some of the streams can be combined?

Specific support is needed to drive the quality, deal with user issues, and constantly adapt the strategy to fit with what users need.

Customization has been discussed in earlier chapters. Customization has great potential, but a lot of people will not attempt it. Instead, they expect the perfect interface magically to appear or just suffer through inefficient processes pushed onto them via the technology.

My recommendation for portals is this: Make sure that there is a strong support group that has typical knowledge intermediary skills outside of technical understanding. You will need an experienced information architect to deal not only with the portal itself but with the underlying information infrastructure that will be the key to the portal being useful. And I would propose to have good ongoing training that not only includes general sessions about what is in the portal and how it could be used, but also personal trainers to help users get the most out of the possibilities that the portal might offer.

OPEN SPACE TECHNOLOGY

The last two tools discussed had a strong technology support component. But knowledge flows most effectively when people are in close proximity. The following is a method that is used specifically to transfer knowledge between people not via remote means but when those people are actually in one room: Open Space Technology (OST). The term technology is actually somewhat misleading as it is more a methodology than a technical concept.

OST is a special method of a gathering (e.g., a meeting, seminar, or even a full conference). But in contrast to traditional events, the organization of an OST event is quite different. The term *open* mainly refers to the agenda. While a traditional event might have a defined agenda with an occasional free-form element, such as a break, an OST event is pretty much the opposite. Topics usually are not chosen beforehand but are brought to the table by the participants. Any interested participants stands up and presents a topic, question, or struggle she has and she is interested in discussing in a group. The main facilitator guides the process to come to a sensible number of those proposed topics. It depends on the number of people in the room, but, for example, for a group of 30 people, you might have four or five topics. Each person who proposed a topic will move to a table, usually in the same room, and put up a sign to indicate what the original topic at that table will be. Participants then swarm out to the tables to form groups of equal sizes.

One interesting rule is that people are not bound to stay at a table but can change tables whenever they like. They can also take a break, if they feel like it. (For more information on Open Space Technology, there are a number of books and articles.)[4]

From a knowledge flow management point of view, OST events are very effective. One prerequisite for effective knowledge sharing is that people are eager to discuss a topic that they are strongly interested in. Within the OST format, the likelihood that those really interested in a topic come together is much higher than in other forms of knowledge exchange.

Participants change tables to make sure they are find the discussion beneficial and valuable.

Ideally an OST event starts with some activity to build basic trust between participants, which again makes interaction on a higher level more likely in the groups.

SEARCH

Search is another topic that could take up several books. In regard to an organizational knowledge flow, internal search engines play an important role. What search engines do is provide a quick way into a range of information that has not necessarily been preorganized in any fashion. It can also offer another way to find information apart from browsing. You could, for example, have a range of documents, e-mails, or Web pages that are structured to be browsed traveling via certain dimensions, such as topics, time, or relevance. But browsing is not always the most effective way to search. If hierarchies get more complicated and the number of elements becomes large or if the person searching does not like topical browsing, search will be a better way to find what is sought.

If elements found via search are properly identified and point to those who had the knowledge when producing that specific element, search can also produce a list of pointers to the person with the knowledge. Search engines usually produce a range of challenges to users mostly related to high numbers of result items. From a human side, these aspects need to be taken into account:

- Often it is hard to specify the right context in a way that search results really offer what you are after. There are some attempts to enhance search with semantics to improve the results.

- Most individuals these days rarely scroll beyond the first page of a search result. If the relevant or "correct" information is not on that page, the searcher might actually build knowledge from incorrect or outdated content.

- Results might be removed from proper context. An example would be a document that originally was linked from a Web page. The Web page might give some context, such as a disclaimer or positioning. Finding only the document without that context might lead to misinterpretation of the information it contains.

- The relevance of search results can be influenced by special features, such as highlighting of key words or phrases.

Even a purely technical tool like search requires people who understand the issues, can train others to use it properly, and build an ongoing strategy around it in an organization.

STORIES

There are many ways that stories play a role in an organization. Stories are actually tools that do not need to be introduced; stories are always there already. But there are different ways to deal with them. You could just ignore them, try to fight some of them, or use them strategically. No matter which way an organization chooses, stories will always play a key role in transporting a certain type of knowledge. With stories, it is not so much the information that gets shared but certain principles or analogies that transport a message. A good story always has some meaning that cannot be put into plain informational text, for example.

Some great work by Steve Denning from the World Bank and David Snowden from Cognitive Edge[5] explains how stories apply in a business environment and how they can be used to drive organizational behavior. Stories often prove to be a lot more effective in transporting a message and getting people to act than just presenting these people with information (i.e., in a presentation). I strongly recommend exploring stories further by reading the available literature on storytelling in business.[6]

KNOWLEDGE TRANSFER SESSIONS

In Chapter 5, I discussed that you need to embed knowledge into the organization to make it harder to be lost when certain experts leave. One method that has been used at SAS is *knowledge transfer sessions*. The method is based on a similar method that Rolls-Royce Aerospace had used and that one of its key knowledge management experts shared.

The typical issue: A key person leaves the department, division, or the organization as a whole, and there is not much time between the announcement and the actual last day in the office of that person. How can you get some of his or her knowledge embedded or captured for later use?

Of course, in an ideal situation, you would have several months or even years for people to shadow the expert to transfer some of the knowledge to them, but realistically, the time frames are much shorter. Knowledge transfer sessions are a minimalistic approach to this problem, acknowledging that keeping some knowledge might be better than keeping nothing.

Here are the simple rules:

▪ The person who is leaving, the *main actor*, sits in the front of the room in the *hot seat*. In a small circle around the main actor are between 6 and 10 *questioners* and 1 or more *facilitators*. The facilitator role is very important; the person should be experienced in facilitating discussions and also have at least a basic understanding of the topic of expertise represented by the main actor in order to ask specific questions in case the conversation slows down.

▪ The questioners are the manager, all or a number of key subordinates, and some other colleagues with whom the main actor had ongoing contact with in the job. Questioners should come somewhat prepared with questions. Even if they do not have the time for preparation or are called in at the last minute, they can be of value, though. They should not feel too much pressure to ask only *smart* questions.

▪ The typical session should not be longer than 90 to 120 minutes. If more time is needed, the sessions can be split. But since this is a pragmatic approach, one session might be all the time you can schedule for the person who is leaving and all the other people needed.

▪ The main actor is asked beforehand whether she objects to being taped during the session. If she does not have any issues with that, a small camera should be set up to record the session. If you can, it would be great to have somebody direct the camera to focus on those talking; if not, set it at a wider angle and focus primarily on the main actor.

▪ The session begins by the facilitator interviewing the main actor by saying things like:
  ▪ Please describe a typical daily routine of tasks you would perform in your job.
  ▪ Tell us about what you liked most about your job.
  ▪ Tell us about those things you liked least about your job.

  At any time, questioners are encouraged to ask qualifying questions, bring up special cases, or ask those things they always wanted to know but never got around to ask.

The main actor is also encouraged to tell stories from the most memorable cases she encountered.

The questioners can then go on to ask questions they had written down beforehand or those that come up based on things other people say.

I have personally facilitated a few knowledge transfer sessions and was always amazed at the depth of the discussions and the astonishingly positive atmosphere that could be created.[7] Questioners found the sessions very valuable and were surprised at how much they learned in the short time frame. It is also amazing how, in almost all those cases, the main actors were positively surprised by the event. Talking about all the things they have achieved and done, making some of their knowledge more visible to themselves and to others, produced a mix of positive feelings. Often others are surprised at the range of things that the actor had to deal with. Usually people do not get time to present themselves in stories and experience sharing, not even for one to two hours.

Other than the camera, there is no technology involved for the actual session when using this tool. If the actor agrees, the recordings can be cut into sensible and easy-to-digest chunks and made available to successors or new colleagues.

As the examples in the previous sections showed, tools can range from technical to people oriented, but even with technical tools, the key is to find ways to use them to really enhance the knowledge flow and not just become information graveyards.

Some of the tools discussed in this chapter (CoPs, skills management, Open Space, and stories) can provide business benefits to organizations by enhancing the degree to which knowledge can flow directly between staff. Other tools (knowledge bases, portals, or search) provide benefits by allowing larger scaling or offering collections of pointers to the one who knows. In both cases the increased knowledge flow can have considerable positive effects.

NOTES

1. Appendix B lists some of my favorite books regarding those tools.
2. Locking would mean taking away the possibility to remove them.

3. RSS (Really Simple Syndication) offers the possibility to address a stream of information (usually produced in an XML format) very easily via a fixed address—a specific type of Web address or URL. The key is that the stream might change in place but is immediately fed to all the places on the Web that have created a link to that address.

4. For an example see Harrison Owen's book *Open Space Technology: A Users's Guide* (San Francisco, CA: Berrett-Koehler, 2008)

5. See Stephen Denning's book *The Springboard: How Storytelling Ignites Action in Knowledge-Era Organizations* (Woburn, MA: Butterworth-Heinemann, 2001) and some articles on narrative by Dave Snowden at www.cognitive-edge.com/articlesbydavesnowden.php

6. A more recent book on storytelling from Stephen Denning is *The Leader's Guide to Storytelling: Mastering the Art and Discipline of Business Narrative* (San Francisco, CA: Jossey-Bass, 2005)

7. You would organize these events only with people who leave the organization under friendly conditions. Be careful with highly frustrated individuals who are not able to keep to business-relevant topics.

CHAPTER 8

Measure and Analyze

On two occasions I have been asked, "Pray, Mr. Babbage, if you put into the machine wrong figures, will the right answers come out?" I am not able rightly to apprehend the kind of confusion of ideas that could provoke such a question.

—Charles Babbage (1791–1871), mathematician and inventor of the first automatic calculator, published 1864

Almost everybody who considers a knowledge flow management initiative very quickly arrives at the topic of measuring. The thought process is usually straightforward. A typical statement I have heard is "You only get what you measure." Those that manage an initiative often believe they can motivate people to participate by creating measures, assigning some targets and just ensuring that the targets are met. But measuring is a more complicated topic than you might think at first; it seems to be one of the topics that people have not found really good solutions for.

There are a number of issues that I have encountered with measuring:

- It is difficult to find meaningful measures for judging knowledge flow management initiatives.

- It can be easy to drive some behavior but very often it is not necessarily the right behavior.

- Trying to measure exactly is difficult, as a lot of the things involved with knowledge are fuzzy and not easy to grasp with hard, fully quantifiable measures.

- Measures can easily be deceiving. They might satisfy the need of having "a measure," but if you dig deeper, you will find they do not measure anything meaningful or it is rather easy to cheat.

In early discussions with other experts, I almost came to the conclusion that you should stay away from measures in knowledge management altogether. But over the years I found there are actually some ways in which measuring can bring value, if you measure with the right expectations and go about interpreting results in a cautious and balanced way. Moving away from my early position of "If you can't measure exactly don't measure at all," I decided to start with "Why not measure just to see some approximate figures and see where it might lead?"

Typical measures used for systems that collect contributions from individuals for others to reuse are contribution and usage numbers. And we used those for our initiatives as well. Some lessons we learned around those measures include:

- **Contribution numbers.** Numbers are only one aspect of contributions. Another one is quality. Be careful not to think that more is necessarily better. But to some degree, contribution numbers can actually be interesting. For one, they are an indication of participation if put into the proper perspective. In the case of ToolPool, it might not say much if there are three or five contributions per month from a given country, but if this number is considerably higher or lower than all the other countries, it can be a useful indicator. Also a relationship over time (i.e., increasing/decreasing) can be a useful indicator. The tricky part is to choose meaningful targets. One way to do that is to set targets at certain averages. In general, as getting people to contribute can be difficult, you usually want more, not less, contributions as long as the quality is right.

- **Usage numbers.** With usage numbers, you have to look very carefully at what "usage" really means. In the case of ToolPool, it is very hard (and would be rather costly) to determine if a certain tool has actually been applied, to what degree, with what success, and producing what value. The lowest level that is possible to determine fairly easily is whether somebody has downloaded a tool. Downloading does not mean it has been used, though. Even if it was used, you would not know the produced value until you analyzed each usage in detail. As mentioned, this can be costly, and obtaining that kind of information could inhibit the actual process in such a way as to cut into normal productivity. But similar to contribution numbers, you can look at usage numbers in relative terms: usage per organizational unit, usage over time, and so on. One interesting relationship I have found over the years is that usage over time drives contribution. I believe this is true for these reasons:
  - If people use contributions, they realize that even simple contributions can be very useful to them and that they themselves might have something of similar value to offer.
  - There is an element of competition and belonging. When people see that many others contribute, they do not want to be left behind, so there is a certain peer pressure. This can be driven further by making competitive numbers transparent, as mentioned earlier. Also, when people use many of the entries and experience their usefulness, they become more likely to feel that it is their time to give something back to the community.

Looking at usage numbers in detail is important to see not only if there is actually reuse participation but also if there is a chance that contribution participation will increase. And if contribution is driven on usage, it is more likely self-driven participation, which often produces higher-quality contributions than would be driven by bonus plan components.

One key fact that we learned was that you should use a balanced approach of measures. Contribution or usage numbers should be part of a more balanced collection of measures that includes softer measures like the process measures discussed in the following section. While contribution or usage numbers in themselves might be dangerous to interpret as a sole indicator for the performance of a knowledge flow management initiative, as part of a more balanced approach, they can actually be of value.

Some years back I actually started to take the usage measure and tried to relate it to a value figure for ToolPool, just to get an estimate. I decided to combine usage numbers with some survey data and some assumptions that I tested in numerous discussions with colleagues around the world.

In a survey we asked users to what percentage they at least once used a tool after downloading it from ToolPool. The average that came back was something a little higher than 25 percent. I then made an assumption that every real usage would save a consultant about four hours. Discussions with project managers, consultants, and others confirmed that this number is quite conservative, as in many cases the savings can be counted more in days than in hours. Because I wanted to stay on the very conservative side with my estimates, I stuck to the four hours. Then I did another conservative estimate about the cost of an hour of a consultant's time, based on internal cost, which was about €100 at the time. Again, this is conservative because it does not take additional opportunity costs into account. As it turns out, that was actually all I needed to do to get the type of minimum estimate I was after. If every fourth access ends in a usage and that usage saves four hours at €100 (total €400), it means that, on average, every access saves €100.

Before I presented that formula to anybody, I had numerous discussions with a range of people, both internal and external, and asked them to shoot holes in it. One early, very good comment was, of course, that I did not take the cost of running the initiative into account. So I did a conservative (high) estimate of costs for support and contribution efforts. With about one tool/day and an average effort to prepare and process a contribution of about eight hours (€800) and a fixed cost for the ToolPool team of about €150,000 per year, this amounted to about €430,000 per year. In contrast to about 75,000 downloads, which amounts to savings of about €7.5 million, the return of investment was definitely on the positive side.

How conservative the estimate is becomes clear when you look at what I call the gut feeling factors. Those are additional elements that I know are there but are very hard or costly to quantify exactly, so I did not account for them in the original formula:

- If somebody downloads a tool and passes it on to one or more colleagues (something we know from interviews and anecdotes happens quite often), we do not count that as a download. It will be on top of our numbers.

- A situation where somebody provides a tool and somebody else provides an improvement that is a value-add is not accounted for.

- A number of ToolPool tools end up as part of developed products or will be turned as a whole into a new product. This can save considerable funds for development. We have not quantified this so far, but the value could be quite extensive.

- Through a global exchange of tools and by making use of the collective knowledge of all our consultants, SAS can satisfy customer requirements faster and draw from a wider pool of innovations. This results in higher customer satisfaction and consequently higher sales.

Based on stories and personal feedback from users, I know all those gut feeling factors are there and provide additional value on top of the basic calculation. But even with the conservative calculation, there were 770,000 accesses in total for ToolPool that have saved the company over €70 million over the years—all costs deducted.

The results were surprising when I first did the calculation. Since then I have used these calculations mainly to show tendencies and make it clear that there is considerable value in such a focused initiative.

More generally, measures and the visibility of value can help to build the business case that is needed to get ongoing initiative funding. Be careful not to expect this type of business case to be a self-runner. You will need to deal with a number of other factors, such as company strategy and politics.

MEASURE TO GET WHAT YOU WANT

One key to measuring is to look at measures not only in isolation. You should create a list of measures that, taken together, give an indication of the performance of a given knowledge flow management initiative. In fact, you actually should go a level higher and score multiple initiatives together into a collected scorecard. The measures can include simple direct measures, such as contribution and usage, but they should also include some indirect measures that by themselves might not be clear indicators of performance but have an indirect influence based on experience. Some examples include:

- Process measures that cover these questions:
  - Do the personal performance reviews include knowledge-sharing behavior components? This by itself will not ensure positive behavior, but the fact that it is a topic twice a year during review discussions raises awareness.
  - Do job descriptions clearly spell out that knowledge-sharing activities are part of the responsibilities? Again, by itself, this might not change much, but it gives those employees who want to spend time on it a way to argue for the activity or managers who want to improve a person's knowledge-sharing behavior a discussion argument.
  - Are their departmental, divisional, location-specific knowledge exchange or transfer events done on a regular basis?
- International measures could cover questions like these:
  - What is the participation rate of a given suborganization at international knowledge exchange events? To what degree is a country participating in global communities of practice (CoPs)?
  - What is the level of involvement in international expert exchanges, such as the resource-sharing process mentioned earlier?

Taking a number of measures (and for your organization those might look quite different) and looking at them from a more balanced view can provide a much better indication of performance than focusing on single measures only.

In my experience, the statement "You only get what you measure" might be true to some extent, but you have to be careful to "get what you want," as individual badly chosen measures can drive people's behaviors very easily in unwanted directions.

In general, it is very hard to measure the actual flow of knowledge, as knowledge that presents high value will exist only connected to humans. And measuring the flow of information does not give a complete estimation of the knowledge that can be created from the information being transferred, as that is connected to prior experiences of the recipient.

That is why most of the time a measure will be more of an indicator of a potential knowledge flow, not a direct quantification. From my experience, these categories of measures play a role in knowledge flow management:

- **Participation measures.** System contributions and usages, attendance and frequency of action (i.e., in a collaborative Web site).

- **Value measures.** Time saved; money earned by using a contribution obtained via a knowledge flow management initiative; portion of sales income secured based on using prior experience; patent revenue and other value driven through an innovation based on knowledge created with the help of a given initiative.

- **Cultural measures.** Indicators that show a cultural shift toward participants being more open and willing to share their knowledge. This might be a measure showing to what degree local staff are turning to a global CoP instead of trying to solve all problems locally.

- **Quality measures.** Measures that look into completeness or format. Beyond that, measuring quality is very tricky, as I discuss in more detail in the next section.

Some of the dangers with participation measures have already been discussed. Let us have a look at value measures for a moment. With the exception of patents, value measures are not easy to quantify. To get accurate figures, you would have to be very diligent and detailed about trying to assess the application of what is being reused. To do that with an initiative that has many entities flowing could involve high costs. Some of the exchange could be easily visible (if a system is involved), but the actual knowledge flowing from person to person is usually considerably less visible. So while it might be possible to assess that value for a selection of entities, it is likely to be costly, take too much effort, and has a danger to intrude on well-running business processes. Some participation measures can be assessed only by detailed questioning of the involved parties.

One solution could be to do somewhat representative assessments (i.e., instead of trying to capture the value of all incidents, capture the value of random samples and extrapolate those). For such sampling coming close to being useful, a critical mass of incidents is necessary, which could still represent considerable cost.

One way of sampling is to work with stories and anecdotes. If a few cases represent a high value in savings or other benefits, it could be enough of an argument for keeping the knowledge flow management initiative running. You might produce measures like "At least five documented cases with proven savings of $1 million," for example.

Another issue to be careful about is the allocation of value. If you have a sales case won that is worth $10 million, how much of it can be attributed to some type of knowledge flow management initiative? How much is personal performance by a single salesperson, how much value did the sales support team provide and what is their knowledge based on, and how much was luck?

One way to get better at this allocation process would be to introduce activity-based management, where you analyze business processes along certain activities and not necessarily based on larger block inputs. But even then there will be gray areas that are hard to quantify or assign. This represents another reason why you should be very careful not to base too much decision power on a single measure but instead work with a larger set of balanced indicators.

MEASURING QUALITY

Quality applied to knowledge can be rather tricky, as discussed earlier. People often propose measuring the quality of elements exchanged through a knowledge flow management initiative via ratings of those entities. Theoretically ratings could provide a collaborative way of getting the crowd to judge an entity. In reality, there are some issues, however:

- Often the critical mass of ratings per entity is not given. As a result, there are only very few or even no ratings at all for many of the entries.[1] Ideally, you would want to have many ratings to get a proper median evaluation.

- It is hard to get people to an aligned understanding of the rating process. Often people rate entries on completely different evaluation dimensions (i.e., some rate completeness; some rate it on personal usefulness, which could be quite different from usefulness to a wider audience). In some cases people just complain about the form of an entry, not evaluating its actual content and potential value.

- Rating via a system is usually easy at the time you encounter an entry, as the rating is connected to what you download. But the real value might become clear only when you use it for some time, so there is a time lag between download and the best time for rating. To make the system work, you would have to get people to come back to an entry to rate it, which is often hard to do. We tried to guide people by also putting rating possibilities into places where they might search for similar elements in the future. One thing that people have suggested was to send users an e-mail on the downloaded tool to ask for an evaluation at a later time. What sounds like a great idea could be annoying in practice. Just because you want the rating data, bombarding users with questions about anything they might have used would surely drive a number of users away.

I think that ratings can still be of value but mainly for some limited feedback and not for real value measuring. I would not consider them an actual measuring tool. You could try to do certain rating events to get people to rate more regularly or introduce some point systems, but that actually drives away focus and attention from the actual reuse. After all, the main purpose of those knowledge exchange initiatives is not the rating itself but the reuse of information for the sake of creating new knowledge.

Before moving on to analytics, let me summarize the points on measuring by formulating some recommendations:

- Use a mixture of direct and indirect measures.
- Mainly measure tendencies.
- Use results for the comparison of participation groups, not to make an absolute statement.
- Look carefully at what you are really measuring.
- If you have to disturb the actual sharing process to fully quantify your results, you are going too far. Measuring should be transparent if at all possible.
- Always look very carefully at motives and behavior of those you are trying to influence via the use of measures. A few participants that use the system in unwanted ways could be acceptable, but if there is a considerable amount of people that show behavior not supporting the actual production of value, you will have to adapt or even drop the measures. An example would be that you are driving quantity instead of quality and that more and more participants provide more entries with less quality just to make the measures.

ANALYZE YOUR INITIATIVE

In the previous sections, I did not provide a silver bullet around measuring. As mentioned, it is a tricky topic, and I think it actually needs more research to refine ways on how to best go about it (a topic for another book). But why do you want to measure in the first place? I think the main motivation should be to help you steer your knowledge flow management initiatives. Those are business processes. And like other business processes in your organization (whether they are customer facing or internal), they need proper steering. In order to guide knowledge flow processes properly it is necessary to regularly analyze them. But analytics is more than just reporting and should include forecasting and optimization to really tune the process to ongoing value creation.

At SAS we have a bit of an advantage, as analytics is a company core competency, analytical thinking comes naturally, and we have everything needed at hand, from the right experience and skills to the proper technical infrastructure.

ToolPool has a whole range of analytical components. They start out with simple reporting, such as access and contribution reports in relation to staff sizes in countries. There are overview reports available that present all countries side by side around some parameters. But you also have the capability to create your own analysis with combining a range of parameters (i.e., countries, divisions, departments, years, months, days, weekdays, type of tools, etc.) into an online report and graphic representation of choice. Through forecasting functions, changes can be anticipated and some situations resolved or optimized before they become a larger issue.

Additionally there are easily accessible consolidated overview reports that represent all contributions for a given author together with the number of downloads those contributions might have gotten, the countries that downloaded them, how often, and on what dates. Those *personal contribution overviews* are a great tool to feed back an indication of the value that contributors produce to the rest of the organization. Seeing that their contribution generated hundreds of downloads, from over 50 countries around the world, is a strong argument that symbolizes the type of attention that contributors often like and that makes them come back to contribute again. A wide distribution also indicates a higher chance that the tool influenced and helped multiple suborganizations beyond just local peers, which is where knowledge sharing often stops without a proper global knowledge flow management initiative in place.

Another type of analysis that can produce useful results is day-to-day usage numbers over the full lifetime for a selected contribution. Looking at those results, contributors can actually see if the interest level on any of their contributions is changing and whether an update results in revived interest.

The contributor report brings all this information together into a simple document:

- A list of all contributions for a selected author ordered from highest to lowest usage.
- Individual usage counts and a total usage count over all contributions

■ Dates indicating when the contribution was first provided and when it was last updated.

■ The average rating with a way to drill down into individual ratings and associated comments.

■ A link for every contribution that leads to a chart for daily access rates over the full lifetime of the tool, with a possibility to select subsets.

■ A drill-down from the number of usages to a report that shows the countries or the hosts those usages have been originating from. From the country and host reports it is possible to drill down into specific access incidents with date and time of day data. This is useful to identify cases where a lot of the accesses came from the same office in a short time frame; in other words, to recognize something that appears to be a bit like buddy support. By making the data transparent, this effect of somebody pushing a colleague's contribution can be reduced. Usually the problem is not as bad as you might think, though, if participants have a clear understanding of the business value of knowledge sharing and do not just focus on some given measures.

The effect that analytics can produce is largely dependent on the quality of representation of the results. One good example was the social networking charts produced during the analysis of person-to-person interaction between different departments at a country organization. In that organization we had a department move from one building to another. The buildings were about 5 kilometers (3 miles) apart, and travel between them took about 20 to 40 minutes, depending on the type of transportation (public, taxi, or private car [including finding parking]) used. The department that moved had contacts to a number of other departments in both buildings. The question was how the connectivity with those departments would change with the move. As this was a predictable event (the move was planned over several months), the analysis happened in two steps. About 3 months *before* the move and 11 months *after* the move, we sent out a questionnaire with five questions:[2]

1. How often do you have face-to-face contact with this person?

2. How often do you have e-mail contact with this person?

3. How often do you have phone contact with this person?

4. Do you regularly ask this person for advice?

5. Do you regularly give advice to this person?

The two result sets (before and after the move) were analyzed and presented in the form of network connectivity charts. While some of the findings were rather predictable, others turned out to be a little surprising. The face-to-face contact rates with colleagues who used to be in the same building but were now separated went down dramatically, which is not surprising, given the distance. Interestingly, though, the e-mail contact rate went down almost as much. We would have thought that e-mail would compensate somewhat for the loss of face-to-face contact. Looking at this in more detail, we discovered that people used to meet in the break rooms while getting a coffee; often this type of contact triggered follow-up e-mails with more details of short discussions. This type of follow-up did not happen any more, and the result was an impact on person-to-person e-mail sending.

Another finding was that the advice networks stayed comparatively stable. So if people turned to someone for specific advice, they still contacted their network even after being separated. I suspect that this contact suffered over time as well, but we did not do a longer-term follow-up to prove that.

The results were easy to present. Just looking at the density of the network graphs showed a clear change in behavior visible to management and human resources. As a result, the head of the department that had moved decided to set up some hot desks in the old location, where department members would spend some time to ensure that a certain level of face-to-face time outside of meetings could happen.

This type of social network analysis (SNA) is somewhat intrusive, though. We ran the questionnaire twice. For an ongoing analysis you would have to run it more often, which would probably result in push-back by staff and management as people usually develop something called "survey fatigue." The idea of automatically recording personal contact information, while technically possible, would result in privacy issues.

There is one example were we analyzed networks in an automatic fashion, however. In this case we analyzed the flow of contributions in ToolPool as well as the flow of experts in our resource-sharing initiative. In both cases, we did not need any questionnaires. We could base the analysis directly on data produced by involved systems. For ToolPool, we have summarized data as to how often a specific contribution provided by one country is downloaded from another country. Together with the described parameters of that contribution, we could analyze not just the frequency but also subdivide the network diagrams by products, solutions, and other categories.

In the case of resource sharing, we also have a process tracking system that records what supplier country provides an expert to what requesting country. And for each exchange we record required technical expertise, products, and solutions as well as the type of services requested (consulting, pre-sales support, training).

An example of the use of such analysis is the identification of company specific innovation and expert centers. As it is solely based on data that is tracked transparently, you can run this type of analysis a lot more frequently. As it is performed on a summarized level, privacy issues can be dealt with more easily.

SNA has since become a popular analytics technique for SAS customers as well. Banks and insurance companies are using this method to identify fraudulent behavior. Telecommunications companies use SNA to identify key customers with a high influential connectivity such that they can be targeted with special marketing offers.

There is a whole range of other ways that we use analytics on knowledge flow management initiatives within SAS. Advanced analytics cover a lot more than reporting. While reporting can be of value, it looks at the past. A lot of additional value can be produced by looking into the future. By using predictive analytics, you can actually be a step ahead of the game. Instead of reacting, you can perform what-if analysis trying multiple scenarios. Based on historic data and intelligent models, you can also optimize your key knowledge flow processes.

You need a number of people developing analytical thinking about this type of business process, just as for many other processes. As knowledge flow management has a great potential to provide extensive value, it is a good candidate to be targeted with this type of analysis.

The key, however, is to combine the analysis itself and the correct interpretation of results. Doing this requires the right type of knowledge intermediaries who are highly familiar with the knowledge-sharing process as well as with company culture and human behavior in general. This is yet another reason to invest in proper initiative support.

Most of what was discussed in this chapter so far seems to apply only to larger organizations and corporations. But even in smaller or loosely connected organizations, the need to steer a knowledge flow management initiative will arise. And while such organizations might not have the luxury of an infrastructure to apply any advanced analytics easily, having an ongoing closer look at where the initiative is heading is very important. If you use some type of technology as a core support component of your initiative, it will very likely be Web based. It might be some hosted software or something you have control over yourself. An example might be some collaboration sites based on Microsoft SharePoint. Whatever you are using, it should have some way to get usage and contribution data (if possible with some indication of the location of accesses). You should also be able to export it for further analysis. In the most basic case you might have to turn to a Web master to supply some basic reporting on how support systems might be used.

For the non-technical elements, you might have to turn to quick regular surveys to get an overview of what is happening, what elements and actions within your initiative are working and which ones are not. Services like SurveyMonkey.com make producing simple surveys rather easy and cost effective. The effort is in creating some smart questions where the answers help you get a better understanding of where your initiative is moving, who is participating, what kind of value is produced, and what type of issues or barriers might exist that you need to tackle.

FEED IT BACK

No matter how big your initiative is and whether you are using an extensive technical infrastructure or not, one of the key points of measuring and analysis is the way you feed results back to participants.

In my experience, this process is often overlooked. There are actually multiple stages of measuring/analysis and using results:

1. No measuring/analysis is done.
2. Measuring and analysis are done, but there is no time or no one responsible for even looking at the measures and further interpreting results.
3. Measuring and analysis are done, and the results are interpreted by a small group of technical system support people.
4. The same as number 3, but results are also made available to key initiative support people and management stakeholders.
5. The same as number 4, but a significant part of the results are also made available to the actual users and contributors.

Many initiatives get stuck in the first three levels; if there is a good knowledge support group, they may make it to the fourth level.

However, level 5 is the most important and powerful one. Transparency is a great way to influence knowledge-sharing behavior.[3] Instead of just using the results for yourself, make sure you prepare them and continue feeding them back to users of and contributors to your initiative. You can do so with a special report similar to the one I mentioned for ToolPool. Alternatively you can offer a self-service portal with a range of reports and online analysis capabilities. It depends a little bit on the audience. Some might have the necessary analytic skills; for others this might be overkill. If you are using some type of newsletter or other regular communication vehicle to build the pulse of your initiative, highlighting some analytic results could make a great addition, whether as a special news item or a short presentation at community events.

By making the results more transparent, you can give some meaning to participants' actions, which makes it more likely that participants will be repeaters. You can also appeal to competitive thinking: People do not want to be behind everybody else. Group pressure makes them want to fit in.

Another effect of feeding back the results is that people are more likely to put in effort in the future. If you do surveys, for example, but never distribute any of the results, people will be less likely to respond the next time as they are not sure what happens to the data they provide. If, however, you not only feed back the results but also explain what actions were taken based on participants' input, the effort they put into answering a questionnaire seems more worthwhile.

Apart from the general users, those in the knowledge flow management support group should have a transparent overview of what is going on. Making sure everybody in the support team, not just management is aware of results as a way to help people motivate themselves. Seeing that their hard work actually results in reuse and people helping each other again and again sends a strong message. Paired with stories, these numbers can paint a picture of the degree of enablement that they are providing to the organization. Especially in the beginning, it is also great to see participation grow. When ToolPool started to pick up country by country, we were always joking that we would be going for "world domination." It was great to see office by office believing in the value of the initiative and integrating it into their business processes.

When it comes to measuring and analyzing, remember not to hide your analysis and results to a small group but use them to show all participants what is happening.

NOTES

1. Even on Amazon.com, where the potential audience to rate books is very large, you will find many books where you are encouraged to become the first one to rate them.
2. We sent the questionnaire to all staff within the selected departments and presented them with a checklist showing everybody but themselves. About 90 percent of those targeted actually participated.
3. As Richard H. Thaler and Cass R. Sunstein discuss in *Nudge: Improving Decisions about Health, Wealth and Happiness* (New York: Penguin, 2009), it is actually a strong influential force for all types of human behavior.

CHAPTER 9

Knowledge Flow Management: The Next Generation

It's tough making predictions, especially about the future.

—Robert Storm Petersen, 1884, Danish writer and cartoonist

What will knowledge sharing look like over the coming decade? Will more companies make the step from looking at it primarily as a technical topic to a more holistic discipline? Will they make the step from knowledge management projects to knowledge flow management initiatives?

To see what might be next, it is worthwhile to look at the developments over the last few years—specifically the role of the Web and those developments (technically and socially) named under the umbrella term *Web 2.0*.

THE ROLE OF WEB 2.0++

There are a number of definitions of what Web 2.0 is, where it starts, and where it ends and something else starts. There is already talk about Web 3.0 and so on, so we might refer to it as Web 2.0++.

To say exactly which concepts and technologies were Web 1.0 and which ones were Web 2.0 is hard, and I will leave that discussion to others. It is not necessarily technical features that define the difference. Some of the technologies that now make headlines have been around longer than many people think. The technical possibility for user-editable Web pages, for example, were there for a while, but only the very easy interface and concept of a Wiki made it spread like it did. And with the clear benefit of a huge encyclopedia available to everybody for free, millions became familiar with the basic Wiki concept. From there it was a logical next step to get a good critical mass of users putting in the extra effort of actually providing content as well.

So, what is the big difference from a knowledge flow perspective, since we have blogging, podcasting, community sites, and much more?

A knowledge flow lives and dies with participation. And that is where a lot of those concepts fit. Making it easy to get away from consumption of static Web pages to participation was a major step forward. The motivation for people to get involved and participate on such a large scale was what surprised many. In some ways open source was a key development that pushed this. The development of Linux as a computer operating system and similar efforts with thousands of developers providing their knowledge for free to create something together was first limited to technical people. But it turned out once you make participation even easier, you could wake that same spirit of providing knowledge to a lot of other and growingly nontechnical areas. People are now helping each other in online forums on anything from buying a digital camera to cooking that perfect Irish stew.

Another success factor is the decentralized character of participation. Even in early Web applications, there could be multiple people involved and participating, but it was usually from a central perspective. They would have to have some type of access to the central place. Things were centrally controlled. The "Web site" was holy; only selected people were allowed to touch it. In Web 2.0, this has changed dramatically. The Web site is only an anchor for people to add, modify, and remove content. Everybody is an actor. And the function of those handling the main site (such as Wikipedia or Twitter) is to make participation easy for everybody but otherwise keep in the background. Keeping in the background does not mean, however, leaving it alone. Instead it means to steer it, to do some viral marketing, and to get a growing community involved, until you pass the bootstrap phase, where you have a lot of supporters helping you spread the message and scale up.

So even with Web 2.0, the technology is only the enabler. The power is with the people, decentralized, direct, and often ending in a person-to-person exchange. Great examples for the decentralized aspect are the community sites such as LinkedIn, Xing, and Facebook. In the old days you would have a phone book at some point including people's e-mail addresses. But with a more globalized world and people moving around a lot, it became harder and harder to keep phone books up to date. People move and the link you had to them (e.g., a phone number) would change. But the need to inform all your friends and former business contacts about that change are over. Community networks were the solution. All you keep is a link to those you want to keep in your virtual phone book. The detail data are kept up to date, not by you but by them. So if five years down the road you want to contact a person, she will have updated her telephone number, e-mail and street addresses, and so on. And maybe she also added a Skype account so you can just push a button, launch your video camera, and have an almost lifelike conversation with her in seconds.

While there are many other effects of social communities, for me this was a strong argument to get started. A number of companies and universities have moved their alumni networks onto those well-known platforms, saving a lot of effort and money over trying to manage alumni contact details internally, a fight they were losing.

What is on the horizon? There is some talk about Web 3.0 already. For some it will mostly be about wider usage of semantics in a way that data is combined with extra information (metadata) clarifying the meaning of that data. As the metadata is passed along with the data it opens up more possibilities for automatic data exchange and integration. For others the key is cloud computing, where the web becomes even more the computer and data and programs are located remotely. I think those concepts and supporting technologies are definitely on the rise, and they will help with some of the scaling issues. In the case of cloud computing, it can extend the "everywhere connected" movement. Instead of dragging your data around, you just keep it in one place—the nebulous cloud—and attach to it from a range of devices, wherever you might be. To be honest, I am not sure, if that really is such a revolution that it deserves the 3.0 version tag.

Instead, I think those and other developments will open up opportunities for additional inventions that together with certain social and human behavior changes might really be revolutionary, and those might deserve to be seen as making up a new version. Whatever that version is, it will influence the knowledge flows on the Web and, with some delay, within organizations as well.

SOCIAL MEDIA INTERNALLY

Over the last few years I observed a general trend that social media tools and processes were moving from the external Web into organizational settings and then were described via the term *Enterprise 2.0*. This is a natural trend as people who are used to certain applications and services when they interact with the Web in their nonbusiness time come to expect a similar experience in their workplace. And in some cases the line between business and nonbusiness blurs somewhat. There are a couple of issues with moving externally proven technologies into an internal setting, however. These are best illustrated using an example.

Tagging or social bookmarking is a technology-based concept where a number of people use keywords (provided via selection lists or free-form as they spring to a user's mind) to categorize, or "tag," content. The items being tagged could be news items, Web links, and more. Good examples are digg.com, reddit.com, and Delicious.com.

The concept of digg.com, reddit.com, and Delicious.com seems like a great candidate to consider for integration into a business environment, and they do have the potential for supporting the knowledge flow. The basic idea is not so much to share the content itself but to share pointers to the content. When a larger group of people votes on certain pointers, these will end up high on the list and supposedly represent the most valuable items.

A few issues need to be hashed out to make this work within organizations:

- It needs a certain amount of scaling and participation. The value that you see on an external scale with a very large audience might not be as high within an organization of 10,000 people, where many still do not see the point.

- I am a strong believer that those technologies also need a "lead" (i.e., investment in a person/team) that will really look after them from an initiative point of view. The build-it-and-they-will-come strategy is not enough. People often think that this is what happened out on the Web, but if you look closer, there is always at least a small group of dedicated, super-enthusiastic folks behind successful implementations based on the technologies. Because these technologies are viewed as self-running, it can be a challenge to get the funding for those resources.

- There is no such thing as a free lunch. That is, even if the tool might be open source, you will need information technology support resources for it, so you will need a proper business case before you invest in it.

- The business model for the companies offering the supporting technologies often goes like this: First offer it on the Web for free, then launch a "professional version" for a small amount of money. As soon as it is used within organizational settings, start charging more money. If the value is really there, it can definitely be worth it. As the technologies have proven themselves and often are already known by the users from engaging externally, it can be a lot better than trying to rebuild them internally. But sometimes organizations are surprised to find that a free open source project becomes a $1 million investment for 10,000 internal users. And that is not counting the initiative support that I propose to have in order to not make that $1 million investment a pure waste of money.

WHAT ABOUT 2020?

Recently I learned about a business school creating courses for *community managers*. A few years back we wanted to use that title for one of the people in our group who was managing two communities of practice (CoPs) and also coordinated a registry for another 80 CoPs within SAS. At the time we decided to not use the title as it could create some confusion. In the United States, for example, the term *community* is frequently used for local real-life city organization. So using it for an online community seemed to have the danger of confusing people internally and externally. But in the future this might actually change. I have seen the title come up a few times in the virtual sense lately.

The local community will still play a role, but for many people, especially the younger generation, communities are defined via some online representation. That does not mean that there is no physical representation of it. In fact, one of the interesting effects that I have observed with my college-age daughters is that they actually do not get "lost" in the online community but use it to manage a wide and international physical community. Facebook is used to stay in touch, but meeting physically is still what it is often about. Facebook is the tool for them to keep that level of familiarity and trust that is needed to engage on an intense level. As mentioned, trust is one of the key prerequisites for high-level knowledge exchange to happen. Online communities fill a void that was created when people started to move around the planet more and as deeper relationships became harder to establish and keep.

In that sense an online community (or at least portions of it) can represent a real community that might actually meet. An example would be those who use Twitter to state that they are in a certain place going for a drink in the hotel bar just to see if there is someone in the same hotel interested in spending some time for a chat over a beer.

SPECIAL ROLES AND JOBS

If knowledge is regarded as a very important topic, and the way to leverage it within an organization is a well-managed knowledge flow, then the logical next step should be more emphasis and focus on the roles within knowledge flow management. Thirty years ago, if you talked about *Web designers* or *Web masters*, listeners might have thought of spiders, not of people who play a central role in the day-to-day operation of your organization. And that is true for almost any organization, not just those making most of their sales via the Web. The Web presence even for brick-and-mortar organizations is an important channel for informing customers about the company, products, and services involving them in communities, or getting their feedback directly.

In a similar way, specialization in important key roles in an organization seems to be the next step when a function gets that important. What seems somewhat harder with the roles needed for knowledge flow management is that the type of knowledge that people need in that role spans areas that have been separate for quite some time. The technological and human aspects within organizations are often still far away from each other. Human resources (HR) staff are using some of the technology as well now—HR intelligence and HR portals are getting a lot more common—but to really bring people issues and technology issues together needs a special skill set that spans those disciplines. So it will need daring organizations to create and support those types of roles, hire the right experts for them, and actually acknowledge their value to the organization by not putting them down as some sort of administrator but recognizing what they often are: key personnel to guide and manage your organizational knowledge flow. It is essential that educational institutions will need to do their part to provide organizations with well-educated candidates who are capable not only of the right kind of bridgelike thinking but also are equipped with all the knowledge and tools needed to help organizations get their knowledge flow running in an optimal way.

STONE AGE: CREATIVITY LEAP THROUGH COMMUNITIES

In June 2009 some anthropologists from University College London published new findings in *Science Magazine* on the influence of communities in the Stone Age.[1] The anthropologists created mathematical models that indicate that a series of "creative explosions" in human ingenuity during the Stone Age could well be due to larger and more diverse communities coming together.

If you take that thought further, we might be at a similar step in the development of humankind. Where in the Stone Age it was more the move from communities of 20 to those of 200 or 2,000, today it is the move from a few thousands to millions, as what is happening on the Internet at the moment. The scale increase is incredible. Are these large platforms like Twitter and Facebook always used for something intelligent or sensible? Definitely not. But who is to judge what the outcome might be in some cases? The key is to focus on the potential, not on misuses, even if in sheer numbers misuses might outnumber value-producing usages. Just because some people do some really stupid things on those platforms does not mean everything done with them is stupid.

In a few hundred years, an anthropologist might confirm the potential introduced by scale and diversity as another great step in the development of human intelligence. What that means for those looking at organizational knowledge flows is to be open, to experiment, and to be careful not to lock themselves into narrow thinking or inflexible platforms that cannot keep up with process changes and new human behavior.

TECHNICAL INFRASTRUCTURES

What social media introduced was scaling as a success factor for connecting knowledgeable people. Other aspects of Web 2.0 are motivation and participation. Why was it possible, on one hand, to get millions (out on the Web) motivated to participate while, on the other hand, it is a big uphill push to get a couple of project teams to put their documents in one place to share?

First, I believe that most organizations currently still have to be viewed as different from the Web as a whole when it comes to judging success of an initiative. In an organization, people usually view success or failure by the number of people who participate, and 100 percent would be nice, right?

But look at the numbers you get on a successful knowledge flow initiative out there in general Web terms. Out of the 1.6 billion Internet users,[2] if only 0.5 percent would participate in your external initiative, you have 8 million people involved. And if only 0.5 percent of those are really self-driven, motivated, and enough of an expert on a given topic to get involved and invest personal time, you would end up with 40,000 super-motivated stars to push, create the pulse, and drag more people into it.

Organizational settings are on a much smaller scale. So you cannot rely as much on self-organizing principles and coincidences internally. For that reason, you have to add a level of support: the drivership.

From a tools perspective, one class of tools will start playing a larger role in the future: automation. While I am a strong believer that technology cannot solve the knowledge flow problem, I believe that certain types of technologies will play an important enabler role.

Text mining and content categorization technologies will help to build ontologies and taxonomies to support folksonomies. They will need to deal with highly dynamic environments, where static- and human-built taxonomies will not be able to keep up with the speed of change.

Social networking analysis will support the knowledge flow, as in the future Web world (internal, external to organizations, or across boundaries) the network itself defines where knowledge flows. So making them visible and analyzing and optimizing them will be a large part of building environments supporting knowledge flow management.

Advanced business analytics are the enabling technologies to provide the right inflow. Your knowledge flow can be really good, but if the knowledge that people develop and share is based on incorrect, out-of-date information and is missing some key insights, it will be limited. So the underlying information delivery and business analytics capabilities of the organization will play a key role.[3] But innovation and knowledge creation happens not only with those types of technologies. It also happens at the border where technology and humans touch, so one important question on any type of knowledge flow management initiative is about the cut-off point along the human–technology continuum, as discussed in Chapter 1.

The cut-off point is different for different types of knowledge. It will also constantly change; as technology evolves, it will lean more to increased usage of technology. As new questions arise and people get to a higher level, it might also move back to grasp and require more of human intelligence.

But because the answer to this question is constantly changing, the high-level strategic initiative guidance is important. It drives not only productivity but also motivation. If the cut-off point is farther toward human activity, there is more of a burden but also more control for the human side. Moving it too much toward the human side will have negative effects on productivity. However, often humans are still better at sensing business process changes and adapting to them on the fly.

If the cut-off point is more toward the technology end, higher trust in the technology involved is needed. And as more technology is mapping business processes, it needs to be very well aligned to what really happens and also be flexible enough to cope with changing processes. Otherwise, the acceptance of and trust in the technology will be destroyed, and people will actually work around the intended technology support. An example might be the type of undocumented rules that coworkers make up on the fly and use to overcome issues where the technology does not fit the process anymore (or never did for that matter).

There are many cases where people have fully underestimated developments based on certain enabling technologies. The time between the prediction that the world would not need more than a handful of computers to a billion of them was only a matter of a few decades. So to predict the level of change that we might experience in the next decade is a daring task.

Just the fact that the technology is available will not mean it will become an immediate breakthrough success. Multiple factors are needed to get people really motivated to use a technology on a large scale. There were other MP3 players before the iPod and other touch screens before the iPhone, but these Apple products were able to push much bigger waves than the pure availability of the basic technologies. It needs humans to play along, and they must develop that motivation to use them. Nowadays this means the technology will have to come with a certain "coolness" factor. If technology comes with that, you can actually charge higher prices for the same or even less performance. People are getting used to double speed, double pixel, double storage capacity, so it loses its attraction as the single selling argument. This development could shift in other directions in the future. Perhaps in 2020, "cool" will be out again and be replaced by other motivational factors.

One area of technology that is still in major development is that of search. Google currently is the clear leader in the search market, but people are asking for more. There are a number of challengers around. The biggest issue is that the amount of content seems to be growing faster than the advances in search technology. While search engines are a lot better today than they were in the past, they do not seem to be keeping pace with the growth of information to be searched. New search engines attempt to deal with natural language processing,[4] and others propose to add semantic information to provide context. Semantic content can really enhance search results, but I see considerable challenges with the scaling. Producing semantic information without human interaction is still very complicated. Developments in this field are not as far along as some might have predicted. The process still needs a large number of people who are ready and willing to add the semantic information that is needed. It requires effort; successful implementations will need to reduce that effort to such a low level that people feel motivated to spend the effort instead of being stopped by the barriers. There will likely be technological help in the reduction of that effort, but in the end if you want to use the crowd, each individual will decide whether he or she finds it worthwhile to spend that effort.

Another issue that I see is the role that commercial interests will play. In the development of Web-based technologies, some sort of commercial interest has usually helped the development at the beginning. At the same time, however, overreactions of those following commercial interests have also slowed the success at some point. Examples are spam in the form of e-mail, blogging, and microblogging. And just like the speed of distribution increased and the time frame until one of those trends reached wide success decreased dramatically, the time it takes for the "bad guys" to catch up is getting shorter. Technologies that bring ongoing improvements will need to deal with those attacks. They will have to have some principles built into their initiative that makes them less vulnerable for some spam or misuse. In the case of social networks, growing distractions, overuse of advertisement, and problems with spam will lead to people leaving as they find the usage more annoying than beneficial.

One interesting recent announcement was that of *Google Wave*.[5] I find a number of elements about it interesting. Its development is not a big bang; actually, Google had made it available early to a large community of developers, building on the collective knowledge of crowds. The strategy is to go for early access and open and wide distribution. While it has some new ideas, it is not totally detached from what people do everyday with e-mail, for example. It just brings together a number of streams (such as chat, multimedia, video, e-mail, and tweeting) in one place. Thus it is not really revolutionary, but it is a logical evolution. More and more people are using multiple channels anyway, so why not give them a more integrated way of using them? It is not a leap; it is more of a natural step. People like improvement, but at the same time many are hesitant to go for big change. Google Wave could actually become an attractive alternative to omnipresent e-mail.

The other interesting idea with Google Wave is that it is open to the point where any organization can create private internal waves. At least at the time of this writing, it looks as if instead of trying to lock people to a platform it owns, Google is trying to make a concept that others could benefit from successful and widely distributed. Of course, Google will be linking business models to it.

A whole range of additional technologies will play a role in the flow of knowledge in general as well as within organizations. Usually they spread based on the large scale of the Internet and then make it into organizations in a more controlled, supported, and smaller-scale version.

The key will not be the technology itself but the type of support those technologies are introduced with in organizations and how they align with the humans who are supposed to benefit from them.

NOTES

1. See more about this research in this news story: www.npr.org/templates/story/story.php?storyId=104973286
2. This 2009 estimate is based on www.internetworldstats.com/stats.htm

3. For more on the growing role of analytics, refer to Thomas H. Davenport and Jeanne G. Harris, *Competing on Analytics: The New Science of Winning* (Boston: Harvard Business School Press, 2007).

4. An example would be a new search engine named WolframAlpha, which currently positions itself as a long-term project. One of the issues challengers currently have is competing with Google's indexing coverage.

5. Google Wave is an online tool for real-time communication and collaboration. It combines traditional tools like e-mail, chat, document editing, photo and video sharing, and more into one interface. As it is server based, activities like typing or adding content are visible immediately by others. More information on Google Wave is available at http://wave.google.com

CHAPTER 10

Final Thoughts

*When the Master governs, the people
are hardly aware that he exists.
Next best is a leader who is loved.
Next, one who is feared.
The worst is one who is despised.*

*If you don't trust the people,
you make them untrustworthy.*

*The Master doesn't talk, he acts.
When his work is done,
the people say, "Amazing:
we did it, all by ourselves!"*

—Lao-tzu (ca. 551–479 BCE), *Tao te Ching*, Chapter 17.

How can you master knowledge flow management?

If you made it through the book to this point, you might be a little disappointed that I did not provide you with a silver bullet on how to master your organizational knowledge flow. I do not think there is such a thing. But to master anything, you need a lot of practice. And to practice, you first need to get started. So while you might not have gotten a ready-to-run solution, I hope that you take away a range of guiding and key principles that will help to master the flow over time.

Some of the elements that I have mentioned might seem rather simple. In reality, they are not necessarily simple to implement. But you will need to keep most of the elements in mind all the time.

- Never forget the human element of knowledge flow management. Do not get carried away and let technology take the full lead.

- Always be aware that you will need multiple drivers to get those experts in your organization influenced to feed their most valuable knowledge into your knowledge flow. Do not be shy of marketing to influence them.

- If you measure, make sure you know what you really measure and what the influence of using those measures might be. Do not measure anything if you are unlikely to ever analyze and use the results.

- Avoid survey fatigue.

- Do not keep results of measuring to yourself but use them actively to drive participation.

- Make sure to get proper support from your organization that is focused beyond the technology that is in place. Get experts on board and make sure you fill key roles for knowledge flow management support. Do not forget how important those people could be to your organization, so acknowledge the value that knowledge intermediary work might provide, and keep the stars in those roles happy.

These are all just guiding principles. I hope some of the examples that I have provided throughout the book will enable you to translate the concepts to work for your own organizational environment. Not everything will apply directly, but I am sure that you can derive behaviors from them that will enhance the knowledge flow in your organization.

Mastering knowledge flow management will be a continuous process. The underlying conditions are in a constant flux. Your organizational culture evolves based on a number of influences; I hope one of them is the move to a more knowledge-aware organization. Supporting technology changes rapidly and can influence human behavior. Business models and processes can change quickly as well.

The changing environment means it will not be easy to come up with any longer-term solution. Mastering means understanding the core principles, translating them to the currently active environment as well as possible, and being prepared to constantly adapt your approaches to changing environments. So the key issue is not so much mastering the knowledge flow in *today's* situation; it is mastering the adaptation to succeed in *tomorrow's* situations. This can work only through building deep experience with all involved components. Although technical understanding is definitely very important, it is the deep understanding of human behavior and how it relates to knowledge that will make the flow work in the end. By having expertise in your organization that can deal with these complex processes, you will provide a chance to anticipate what might be needed later instead of just reacting to what you see today.

But you are not alone. Just as the more technical-oriented knowledge management has found a growing community, there is a growing group that understands the wider concepts of managing the knowledge flow more holistically.

This book is my attempt to give this movement a little bit of a push, and I am planning to keep with my favorite topic via a dedicated blog. If you have experiences, examples, or comments, I very much welcome them at masterknowledgeflow.blogspot.com.

Key Success Factors

Throughout the book I touched on a number of key factors that will make mastering your knowledge flow more successful. The following list collects those key success factors into a convenient collection. Ordered by general areas of focus they combine important clarifications with specific actions and approaches.

Make sure to have these in mind when approaching any of the areas or pick specific actions to approach issues with your knowledge flow initiatives.

Analytics

- It is not part of knowledge flow management itself but rather an element for knowledge creation.
- It is an important dimension for high-quality knowledge to enter the flow around the organization.
- Develop analytical thinking in the minds of those supporting your initiatives.
- Feed analysis results back to all stakeholders.

Barriers

- Remove barriers to enable a natural knowledge flow.
- Attack barriers at the right level (i.e., from the top).
- The position that "Knowledge Is Power" can be a dangerous personal point of view.

- Acknowledge that sharing knowledge takes effort; reduce the effort but do not expect to reduce it to zero.

- More is not always better—offering too much information will often result in the targeted people skipping the information completely.

- Quality can be hard to judge; small and raw ideas can be more valuable than large complete deliveries.

- Encourage people to contribute to initiatives earlier instead of holding back ideas too long.

- Acknowledge legal limitations and work with legal groups if your organization offers such support.

Executive Buy-In

- Get executives to lead by example.

- Get their ongoing endorsement—not just for the launch.

Feedback

- Make sure to offer feedback to *all* participants.

- Provide regular ongoing feedback as well as occasional interesting facts.

Marketing

- Sell initiatives internally.

- Marketing must be ongoing, not limited to a big-bang launch.

- Create a pulse.

- Use internal and external success stories.

- Reach people via those places that they are currently using.

Measuring

- Measure conservatively, then look at tendencies.

- Carefully design measures—you must be able to measure in a way that does not inhibit the measured business process.

- Use a balance of multiple measures: qualitative and quantitative.

- Be very clear about effects, especially side effects of measures.

- Look at indirect changes—be careful with expecting any positive direct changes from measures.

- Provide feedback results to all participants (contributors, users, support team), not just management.

Motivation

- Financial rewards are poor motivators and usually backfire on you.
- Different people are motivated by different drivers—work with a portfolio of drivers.
- Reduce demotivators to give motivation a chance to develop.
- You cannot tell anybody to be motivated.

Reward and Recognition

- Different participants need different drivers.
- Use a portfolio approach—do not rely on one driver only.
- Design a system of drivers that contains redundancy.

Roles

- Develop special knowledge support roles.
- Build or hire experts to fill intermediary roles.
- Where you cannot build knowledge flow management expertise, buy it or have people obtain it via external communities.
- Anybody can be a sponsor, not just executives.
- Make sure your knowledge intermediaries bring the right mix of passion, service mentality, and human and technical understanding.

Scaling

- Do not underestimate the value that scaling can bring, even within an organization.
- Visualize scaling effects to your key stakeholders.
- Go global—and make sure your environment supports that move.

Support

- Do not limit support to technical support.
- Include usage support.

- Include contribution support.

- Make a similar-size investment in initiative support as in technology.

- Ensure that you have passionate people driving your initiative. Give them ownership and provide them with feedback channels that enable them to see progress.

- Locate your knowledge flow management support team where it can have organizational impact.

- Do not view knowledge flow management as something that can be handled in one project; rather view it as an ongoing initiative.

Systems

- Develop any systems involved in an iterative way, building on intermediate successes as you go.

- Ensure that your systems are designed in a modular fashion. Connect modules intelligently.

- Design your systems architecture to be easily extendable in a way that modules can be added or replaced as new technology becomes available or new needs arise.

- Focus on system flexibility. Business environments keep changing and you will need to be able to easily extend your support systems.

- Teach people to look beyond the system to see that they are also a collection of pointers to the one who knows, not just a repository of assets.

Web 2.0

- You need proper support; Web 2.0 and social media are not self-running, even though they might seem so.

- Do not underestimate cost and effort to transfer externally successful platforms into internal settings and get them succeed in smaller-scale environments.

APPENDIX **B**

Additional
Resources

Collison, Chris, and Geoff Parcell. *Learning to Fly: Practical Knowledge Management from Leading and Learning Organizations*. Oxford: Capstone, 2001.

Davenport, Thomas H., and Jeanne G. Harris. *Competing on Analytics: The New Science of Winning*. Boston: Harvard Business School Press, 2007.

Davenport, Thomas H., and Laurence Prusak. *Working Knowledge: How Organizations Manage What They Know*. Boston: Harvard Business School Press, 1998.

Denning, Stephen. *The Springboard: How Storytelling Ignites Action in Knowledge-Era Organizations*. Boston: Butterworth-Heinemann, 2000.

Gladwell, Malcolm. *Blink: The Power of Thinking Without Thinking*. New York: Little, Brown, 2005.

Gladwell, Malcolm. *The Tipping Point: How Little Things Can Make a Big Difference*. New York: Little, Brown, 2000.

Heath, Chip, and Dan Heath. *Made to Stick: Why Some Ideas Survive and Others Die*. New York: Random House, 2007.

Rumizen, Melissie Clemmons. *The Complete Idiot's Guide to Knowledge Management*. Indianapolis: Alpha Books 2002.

Surowiecki, James. *The Wisdom of Crowds: Why the Many Are Smarter than the Few and How Collective Wisdom Shapes Business, Economies, Societies and Nations*. New York: Doubleday, 2004.

Tapscott, Don, and Anthony D. Williams. *Wikinomics: How Mass Collaboration Changes Everything*. New York: Penguin, 2008.

Thaler, Richard H., and Cass R. Sunstein. *Nudge: Improving Decisions about Health, Wealth and Happiness*. New York: Penguin, 2009.

Wenger, Etienne, Richard McDermott, and William M. Snyder. *Cultivating Communities of Practice*. Boston: Harvard Business School Press, 2002.

About the Author

Frank Leistner is Chief Knowledge Officer in SAS Global Professional Services. He has been in the information technology industry for over 20 years, starting as a systems programmer for Nixdorf Computer in his home country of Germany and working from 1989 to 1993 for Siemens-Nixdorf in a liaison role out of Mountain View, California, where he focused on the development of UNIX multiprocessor operating systems.

In 1993 Frank joined SAS in its European headquarters, focusing on application development and field consulting. Based on experiences in the field, he founded the SAS knowledge management program in 1997 and has been leading a range of knowledge exchange initiatives with a global scope since then.

Between 1999 and 2003 he worked with the Institute for Knowledge Management led by IBM. In 2003 he was invited to the Harvard Graduate School of Education Learning Innovation Laboratory roundtable. From 2005 on he worked with the Babson Working Knowledge Center led by Thomas Davenport and Larry Prusak, two pioneers in knowledge management.

Frank holds an MSc in computer science from the State University of New York at Albany and a master's degree in computer science from the Carolo-Wilhelma Technical University in Braunschweig, Germany.

Frank provided a chapter in the 2003 book *Leading with Knowledge: Knowledge Management Practices in Global Infotech Companies* (Tata McGraw-Hill) and has written case studies for a number of books published as part of knowledge management and business conferences.

He has presented at numerous conferences and given keynotes in Europe and the United States on knowledge management, talent management, and Web 2.0 topics.

Index